GARDENERS' WORLD
BORDER PLANNING

Over 20 complete recipes to transform your garden

Anne Swithinbank

D1465004

BBC Books

The publisher thanks the following photographers and organizations for their kind permission to reproduce the photographs in this book:

2 Clive Nichols (Vale End, Surrey); 6–7 Jerry Harpur (Chenies Manor); 10 S&O Mathews; 11 Jerry Harpur (Home Farm, Balscote); 15 Noel Kavanagh/designer Beth Chatto; 18–19 S&O Mathews; 22–26 Brigitte Perdereau; 31 Brigitte Perdereau (Ladham House); 34 Clive Nichols/designer Beth Chatto; 38 Eric Crichton (Mrs Una Carr, Bathford); 42–43 Brigitte Perdereau (Ladham House); 43 Neil Campbell-Sharp (Tintinhull); 46 Juliette Wade (Stonewell House); 51 Garden Picture Library/Neil Holmes; 54–55 Jerry Harpur (Tessa King-Farlow, Edgbaston); 59 S&O Mathews; 62 Brigitte Perdereau (Bosvigo Garden); 66 Jerry Harpur/designer Preben Jakobsen, Cheltenham; 67 S&O Mathews; 70 Andrew Lawson (Kemerton Manor); 71 Jerry Harpur (Park Farm, Great Waltham); 74–75 Andrew Lawson (Kemerton Manor); 78 Eric Crichton (Maureen Lewsey, Hythe); 83 Andrew Lawson (Docton Mill); 86 Clive Nichols/designer Wendy Francis (The Anchorage, Kent); 90 Garden Picture Library/Ron Sutherland/designer Beth Chatto; 94 Jerry Harpur/designer Bruce Kelly; 95 Clive Nichols/designer Peter Aldington (Turn End Garden, Haddenham): 98–99 Brigitte Perdereau (Ladham House); 103 Andrew Lawson; 106 Jerry Harpur/designer Beth Chatto; 110 Clive Nichols/designer Beth Chatto; 111 Jerry Harpur (Park Farm, Great Waltham); 114 Brigitte Perdereau (Coach House); 122 Juliette Wade (Will Giles, Norwich); 123 Brigitte Perdereau (Wisley Garden).

Published by BBC Books,
an imprint of BBC Worldwide Publishing.
BBC Worldwide Limited, Woodlands,
80 Wood Lane, London W12 0TT
First published 1996
© Anne Swithinbank, 1996
The moral rights of the author have been asserted

ISBN 0 563 37187 0

Set in Bembo
Printed and bound in Great Britain by Butler & Tanner Limited,
Frome and London
Colour separations by Radstock Reproductions Limited, Midsomer Norton
Cover printed by Clays Limited, St Ives plc

GARDENERS' WORLD
BORDER PLANNING

Contents

Introduction

～

There is nothing so satisfying for a gardener than standing back and admiring a border of plants which really work well together. I view gardening as an art form far more complex than painting a picture or putting a collage together. Plants will grow and change, so that what may look fantasic for three weeks in summer will often be different by late summer and totally changed for the rest of the year. Most of us have small to modest-sized gardens, and need our borders to look good throughout as much of the year as possible – which can take a lot of artfulness and imagination. Although I have divided this book into border themes, I hope that readers will mix and match them to please themselves. A gardener planning to use mixed, low- maintenance shrubs, for instance, may wish to inject seasonal interest here and there using ideas from the chapter *Seasonal Borders*.

Beauty is in the eye of the beholder and, as in any art form, what appeals to one person may appal someone else. Every garden is like a small part of paradise for its owners. It is where they can relax and take delight in growing plants as well as putting them together to create a picture that pleases them. It really does

The permanent plantings of a border can be livened up for spring by adding warm-toned tulips and yellow, scented wallflowers to give a memorable display.

～

not matter what the rest of the world thinks. The designing of borders, then, is personal, so although this book is inevitably the result of my thoughts and feelings, I have tried to temper these with a certain measure of objectivity.

I think we all know what is meant by 'tasteful plantings'. Book shops are full of inspirational tomes written by famous and accomplished gardeners, whose own borders no doubt spill over with a wealth of choice plants. Part of me aspires to this, even when my borders are considerably smaller, but there is also a childlike desire to have fun. I want to shock people who visit my garden and make them gasp with surprise at warty gourds, squirting cucumbers and huge, acid yellow dahlia flowers! I also have to fight a compulsive urge to collect unusual plants, which constantly jeopardize any designs I have in mind.

This book is to give inspiration to those new gardeners who are faced with bare borders and have no idea what to put in them. I hope that by leafing through the chapters, they can at least identify with a theme and get a few ideas of plants which might work well together. The great thing about gardening is that plantings can be adjusted afterwards.

My thoughts are also for those gardeners who have had trouble with an existing border and have decided to attempt an overhaul. The sheer number of cultivated plants to choose from can sometimes be a nightmare rather than a blessing. It may help to draw boundaries by channelling your search towards certain colour combinations, or selecting plants to cope well with an identified limitation like dry shade or a need for low maintenance.

The chapters cover a wide range of themes and I have tried elements of them all in my own garden. My personal favourites include ensuring that all seasons are well represented, with every effort made to encourage and welcome wildlife. I have also become increasingly keen to tailor plants to suit my soil. Gardening then becomes easier and there is a satisfying impression of plants at ease with their surroundings rather than struggling against the elements.

Learning how to identify soil type, carry out plans and decide where to put the plants is vital to success, so unless the reader is already expert in this, a good perusal of the practical chapters at the beginning of the book will be necessary to use the more inspirational information further on.

The most important thing about successful border planting is that plants can be moved, during their first few years if they are shrubby and throughout their lives if they are herbaceous perennials. This can help a prospective border planner to be less anxious about making mistakes. I have to confess that I have never planted a border yet and been totally satisfied with it from the start. I always end up moving one or two plants, then add and subtract quite happily over the years. Being able to learn and change is all part of the fun of gardening.

Border Planning

Once you have decided to create and plant a new border, or take apart an old one with the intention of improving it, there is a temptation to start straight away. The end result will be more organized if just a little time is spent on drawing out the border, more or less to scale, on paper. There are several jobs to do.

1. Draw the shape of the border approximately to scale.

2. Analyse the soil type and decide how it can be conditioned or improved.

3. Consider the aspect and the quality of light received.

4. Make a list of any existing plants and their current position.

5. Plan how the new border is going to look on paper, noting which plants will be retained.

6. Make a list of new plants which will be needed and choose them with care.

1. Drawing a border to scale is not as daunting as it sounds. First, draw a rough sketch of the border. Measure its length and note this on the rough plan. Then do the same with its depth, which may vary. If it does, measure in several places, noting exactly how far apart the measurements have been taken. (This task is much easier if it's carried out by two people.)

Next, plot the position of any mature trees and shrubs which are going to stay where they are in the border. Measure from the back and from the nearest side to get their exact position. Once you're back indoors, this rough plan can be translated into a proper scale drawing of the border. Graph paper makes this job easy. What scale you use will be dictated by the size of the border and how its length and breadth will fit on to the paper. The last time I designed a border, I used graph paper to the scale of 2 cm= 1 m. This made drawing the plants quite easy, as a specimen which ultimately spread to 1 m occupied a 2 cm square.

2. The texture of soil can be determined by grabbing a handful when it's moist. Squeeze the soil together, then attempt to throw it up and down gently a few times. If it crumbles almost straight away, it is light and sandy. If it falls apart gradually after the first or second throw, it is likely to be a good, medium-textured loam. However, if it sticks into a solid ball, it is clay.

The acidity or alkalinity of a soil is important to some plants and can be measured by gauging the pH. Soil testing kits are widely available and will tell you whether the soil is acid, neutral or alka-

Good planning brings winning combinations of colour and texture. Here, oriental poppies and a galaxy of ox-eye daisies shine against silvery Brachyglottis.

line. If it's acid, plant choices can include acid lovers like *Rhododendron, Pieris* and *Fothergilla*. A neutral soil will support most plants except those that need an acid soil. If the soil is very alkaline (chalky), not only will the acid lovers virtually stop growing and show signs of leaf-yellowing, but some others such as *Hamamelis* (witch hazel) which dislike a particularly chalky soil are unlikely to really thrive.

The most sensible advice is to recommend that gardeners choose plants to suit the pH of their soil. Many hanker after an acid soil so that they can grow the many plants which require this as well as those which are not fussy. A comprehensive plant encyclopaedia will indicate plants that must have an acid soil. When growing vegetables, particularly those in the cabbage family, it will be necessary to make soil more alkaline. This can be achieved by dressing it with ground limestone on an annual basis.

When gardening on chalky soils, it seems only logical to choose plants which originate from chalky areas. There are many, including shrubs like *Abelia, Berberis, Buddleia, Chaenomeles, Cistus, Forsythia,* pink hydrangeas, holly, lavender, *Philadelphus,* lilac and *Viburnum. Clematis,* of course, are good chalk-tolerant climbers. When designing a border and compiling the plant list, check each plant in a reference book to make sure it is chalk-tolerant.

Sometimes gardeners are determined to grow acid-loving plants despite having the wrong soil. If planted straight into an alkaline environment, these plants will slowly take on a sickly yellow appearance, largely attributable to iron deficiency. Although special feeds containing iron are available, they can only prolong the inevitable decline. However, there is no reason why one or two acid-loving plants should not be planted into tubs of special ericaceous compost and stood on the border, raised slightly on bricks or pot feet. Adding leaf or pine needle mould to a neutral soil will help lower its pH and make it more acceptable to a wider range of woodland plants which tend to prefer their soil on the acidic side.

3. Aspect is vital, as this will determine whether the border is predominately light or shady. The sun rises in the east and sets in the west, so an east-facing border receives soft morning light, but is shaded in the afternoon. A west-facing border receives bright afternoon sun. A border facing south receives sun for most of the day and that facing north receives little or no direct light.

Observation is the key to understanding your garden. It is advisable to wait a year before beginning any alterations to a new garden and during this time you should note which areas receive full sun and which are in total shade, as

A metallic combination of bugle and Myosotis *with silvery* Arrhenantherum *makes effective underplanting for geranium and paeony in a semi-shaded spot.*

11

well as the in-between stages. Whilst doing this, also note windy areas and those which freeze quickly and stay frozen longest in winter. There may be odd corners which hardly become frosted at all where tender plants or delicate winter blossoms can be tried.

Sun and shade are not only influenced by your garden's aspect, but by any obstructions such as buildings and trees. The effects of these obstructions will also alter at different times of year. During the summer, the sun moves in a high arc and gives much better light than in winter, when its movements between rising and setting are lower and buildings and trees cast longer shadows. The back of my house faces roughly north east and whereas morning light shines right into the back of the house in summer, it is gradually pushed away from the house by shadow as the sun gets lower in winter. By midwinter, we receive no direct light downstairs at all as the windows are shaded by walls and hedges. Plants growing against the house have to be able to cope with this.

4. Apart from trees and shrubs too old to be moved, it is likely that the remaining plants will be removed, or at least lifted out of the way and heeled in elsewhere. Even if they are to be retained, it is unlikely that you will wish to compromise the whole new design by leaving them where they are. This presents an ideal opportunity to condition soil. I usually single dig, which can be difficult if the border is an odd shape. Tackle it in rectangular chunks, digging a trench one spit (spade depth) deep across one end. Put the spoil into a wheelbarrow and use it to refill the last trench. In between, it is simply a case of forking over the base of the trench spreading well-rotted compost or manure inside, adding a dressing of fertilizer, then turning the next strip of soil over to fill the trench, using a spade.

5. Planning the new border will depend on what general idea or theme is to be followed. However, every border needs a backdrop of some kind. In many cases there will be a hedge or fence with a mature wall of greenery behind. If there is little there at all, it may be necessary to plant a hedge, cover a naked fence with climbers or furnish the back of the border with tall plants to provide a background.

Start by planning the backbone plants – those trees and shrubs which will form the main character of the border for many years. Then add smaller shrubs and herbaceous perennials, to make weaving contours throughout. Finish off by adding ideas for areas of bedding plants, vegetables or bulbs if they are to be included. Incorporating existing plants which were rescued from the old design will save money. Where borders are deep, it can be fun to add one or two plants to rise up as features from the middle ground. The standard rose featured in the photograph on page 114 is a good example, or you could use statuesque plants like tall verbascums.

These plants can be drawn on the plan as informal blocks to show their spread. Where more than one plant is to form a group, mark the individuals with a cross to indicate numbers. There has to be a compromise between young, immature plants and the size they will eventually reach. With the backbone plants, I believe in taking their ultimate size into consideration. The gaps between them can easily be plugged by a succession of smaller plants with shorter lives. With herbaceous perennials, plant between one and five of them to make a group. They grow quickly, so it is possible to economize by planting one initially and waiting a couple of years for it to grow into a large clump which can then be divided into several. In the interim, gaps can be plugged with annuals so there are no bare patches.

It is worth noting at this point that repetition is a useful tool with which to bring a long, potentially disjointed border together. One of the backbone shrubs can be repeated at intervals down the border – roses are effective when repeated and so are bold groups of herbaceous perennials. Where a firm edge is required, either plant a low hedge of box or lavender to retain more informal plants, or use a regular pattern of low-growing, bold plants.

During the early stages of a brand new border, where all the plants are young and small, it is possible to inject some shape and style in a number of ways. First, it may be worth buying a few years' growth by investing in one or two larger plants. Another idea is to use structures like obelisks or woven willow teepees for climbers. Annuals, like sweet peas, will quickly make these a feature and they look just as good bare in winter. Or you could make a short path into the border leading to a small, paved area to act as a hard standing for an urn or bench. The entrance can be marked by a pair of small, formal shrubs.

6. The obvious place from which to buy plants is a garden centre. Just as you would check the quality of fresh produce at a supermarket, look for healthy, even growth and avoid small plants wallowing in very large pots (usually bad value) and the obviously pot bound. When buying herbaceous perennials, look out for really good potfuls which could be divided straight away into two or three individuals. Never be beguiled by open blooms, but search instead for well-shaped plants with healthy growing points.

There is also a case for widening the net for economy and variety. Good plants can be obtained from small specialist nurseries and by joining groups like the Hardy Plant Society and the NCCPG (National Council for the Conservation of Plants and Gardens), whose local branches frequently hold plant sales (see page 125 for addresses). Try to visit small gardens which are open to the public, as these often have sales benches of plants propagated from unusual stock held in the garden. All over the country, keen amateur gardeners raise and sell surplus plants at bazaars, jumble sales and fêtes. Do inspect these carefully for good health before buying and planting.

Border Cultivation

~

Whether low- or high-maintenance, all border plants need some care and cultivation if they are to thrive. When it comes down to looking after any plant, the skill lies in identifying a problem and solving it before it turns into a disaster. Experience will eventually teach gardeners to anticipate problems and take steps to avoid them *before* they occur, saving time and potential damage to plants.

Planting

Although we are told that container-grown plants can be planted all year round, I prefer to carry this out between September and April when the soil is moist and plants are unlikely to be stressed by hot sun. Many take well from an autumn planting when the soil is still warm. On the other hand, tender plants are best left until spring. They then have all summer and autumn to adjust to the strange climate and soil of your garden before enduring their first winter.

Once the soil has been prepared (see *Border Planning*), set out the plants on the surface in their planned positions. Now is the time to see how well a border design transfers to reality. Be prepared to be flexible and keep imagining what the plants will look like when fully grown. I usually set out and plant the major backbone plants first, then smaller shrubs and herbaceous perennials, working from the back of the border to the front and steadily along the length of it. If there are a lot of bare-rooted herbaceous perennials saved from the old design, avoid setting them out too soon, or their roots will dry out. Use short sticks and labels to mark their positions instead.

A spade is the best tool for planting all but the smallest of bedding plants, which can be put in with a trowel. Simply dig a hole a little bigger than the plant's root-ball and set the plant in. Make sure it is at the same height as it was in the pot or previous border, digging a deeper hole or placing more soil beneath the roots until this position is found. Only then should soil be pushed back around the roots and firmed in.

Bulbs are usually added after the other plants. It is important to plant them as deep as recommended, which can be 15 cm (6 in) in many cases. Either make individual holes with a trowel (special long thin trowels are available for the job) or, for a group, take out a flat-bottomed hole to the correct depth, place the bulbs inside and infill.

Moving Plants

Even in the most carefully planned borders, it is likely that one or two plants will turn out to be too close and begin to obscure each other or clash. The best time for moving young evergreen shrubs

Well conditioned soil can support double-layer planting. Here, dainty yellow flowers of Bupleurum falcatum *(Sickle hare's ear) thread through orange* Crocosmia.

∼

right through to March, providing the soil is neither waterlogged nor frozen solid. Most herbaceous perennials (plants that last from year to year but, unlike shrubs, do not make lasting woody stems) will not object to being uprooted and moved any spring or autumn, it seems necessary. Some positively thrive on being lifted, divided and replanted every three years or so at these times of the year.

To divide a herbaceous perennial, shake off the excess soil, then push two forks, back to back, into the middle of a clump of tangled roots and prise apart. Alternatively, sharpen your spade (sharpening stones are invaluable for spades and hoes), aim well and chop solid clumps in half, then in quarters and so on.

is during the early part of autumn when temperatures are growing cooler and the soil is usually moist but still warm. This creates ideal conditions for new root growth before the onset of winter. Deciduous shrubs destined for a move should be allowed to drop their leaves first. All trees and shrubs can be moved

Staking

Current thinking has it that young trees should be staked as little as possible, so that they naturally strengthen their trunks against the effect of the wind. This is all very well, but what if you buy a slender tree that actually bends over, as two of my young birches did? They needed slender tree stakes to support their stems. When planting a container-grown tree, position the tree in the hole, then push the stake in on the same side as that from which the prevailing wind blows. To get the stake close enough to the stem, it will be necessary to take a hand fork and gently tease away some of the roots on that side of the rootball. Bare-rooted trees will not have the same problem, as the stake can be pushed in between the roots.

Trees whose stems are sufficiently thickened to stand upright will only need securing to a short stake (say 45 cm/18 in up the stem), to stop their roots from being rocked by wind. With container-grown trees, a stake can be knocked in at an angle to avoid going through the rootball. With bare-rooted trees, simply push the stake between the roots as described before. Tying young trees to stakes requires care. Follow the instructions and check regularly to make sure there is no rubbing or biting into the stem as it grows.

A year after my Irish yew was planted as a 1.5 m (5 ft) specimen, gales pushed it sideways. My solution was to rig up two vertical wooden supports banged into the ground on either side of the roots, with a cross-piece fixed across the top at a height of about 45 cm (18 in). To this cross-piece I secured the trunk firmly with old nylon tights. This contraption proved effective and was not ugly to look at. After three years, the tree was able to stand alone. Sometimes there is no textbook solution, but common sense often provides an answer.

Herbaceous perennials frequently need support, or their stems will be flattened by summer storms. Either learn to avoid those with floppy stems, or build up a collection of specially designed (though expensive) plastic-coated wire structures,

pea sticks of hazel or birch, or canes and string. These need to be put in around the plants when they are still young and growing. Pea sticks should be pushed in around the plants. Then have their tops bent down and in towards the centre, crab-pot fashion. If using canes, push them around the plants and tie string round them. Stems will grow through and become supported, while hiding the supports themselves.

Watering

If no effort has been made to choose drought-tolerant plants, and a border is in full sun, extra watering will be needed during summer droughts. This is particularly important while plants are establishing. Water them during the evening, or early morning and make sure the roots get a good soak. Simply spraying water at the leaves will do little good; it is the roots under the leaves at which water should be aimed. Automatic irrigation systems including seep hoses will make the job of watering far easier, and use water more economically. If there are hosepipe restrictions, water used for washing vegetables, or even washing-up water (but not too greasy) can be used. Target thirsty plants and put plenty on at any one time.

Feeding and Mulching

I like to add a slow-release fertilizer to my borders in the spring, then, while the soil is still moist, put on a 5–8 cm (2–3 in) thick mulch. This can be of well-rotted compost (make sure it does not contain weed seeds, or roots of nasty perennial weeds like couch grass or ground elder), well-rotted manure, mushroom compost (though not where lime-hating plants are growing), or any other proprietary soil conditioner. Nutrients are added naturally to the soil, weeds are suppressed if the mulch is put on 5–8 cm (2–3 in) thick and moisture is retained.

By and large, over-feeding shrub and herbaceous perennial borders is a mistake. Growth becomes lush, sprawling and shows little drought tolerance. The only plants to which I would give additional liquid feeds are bedding plants, which can take a general-purpose fertilizer every fortnight to encourage flowering. Unless the soil is very acid, lime-hating plants like *Rhododendron* and *Pieris* will benefit from a specially formulated liquid feed containing iron.

Weeding

Freshly turned soil always sprouts a crop of weeds, so do not be perplexed if a newly planted border suddenly produces a mat of weed growth. Regular weeding to prevent them from seeding will work. Perennial weeds left in the soil from previous plantings, or creeping under the hedge from next door, can also be kept at bay by regular rooting out.

There are weed-suppressing mats which can be spread over the whole bed before planting. Holes are cut to accommodate plants and the whole process is made more fiddly, but the mat is then concealed by a thick mulch and weeds are smothered.

Regular border weeding can be under-taken with a hoe, which saves time, but forfeits the chance to save seedlings of desirable plants.

Pruning

As they mature, the growth of flowering shrubs can be kept under control by pruning. Those such as *Forsythia, Philadelphus* and *Weigela* are best pruned straight after flowering, so that they can immediately make new growth on which blooms will open the following year. This pruning is a matter of common sense and an eye for shape. The same principle can be applied to almost any kind of shrub that needs thinning or reducing in size. Carefully cut out older stems which are not well placed, taking out up to one third at a time. Cut these close to the base, or to where a promising new shoot is sprouting.

Some shrubs, like *Cornus alba, Salix alba* and *Eucalyptus*, can be stooled. This means that every year, in spring, the stems are cut down to within short spurs of older wood. From these spurs of younger wood, buds grow into a rash of young stems.

Unless a clipped, formal shape is desired, do not reduce size by cutting informal plants to a desired height. The shrub will respond by growing from the cut ends, resulting in strangely shaped, artificial-looking plants which are unlikely to flower.

Young hedge plants may need help to bush out. Do not start clipping until growth has gone just beyond the desired height or width. Formative pruning consists of reducing the length of long shoots by about two thirds. This will make them branch, resulting in a thicker hedge.

Low-maintenance Shrub Borders

～

However much you may long for burgeoning herbaceous borders, brilliant bedding plants or pretty potagers of fruit, vegetable and flowers, this is hard to achieve unless regular time can be spent in the garden. However, with careful planning, interesting and well-furnished borders can be maintained by planting shrubs which knit together to make a dense tapestry of leaves. Once plants are established, their roots penetrate deep into the soil and become reasonably drought tolerant. The soil itself is shaded and few if any weeds are able to grow under the dense shade.

For those who cannot spend much time gardening, this type of low-maintenance gardening is a boon. Shrubs are interesting and varied enough so that gardeners can exercise their horticultural muscle without involving a lot of work. Once shrubs are established, their shapely contours repel children from stepping on borders and even footballs seem to bounce off the foliage, causing

Proving that foliage can be as much fun as flowers, this imaginitive planting of shrubs has knitted together to make weed-suppressing mounds of colourful leafy growth.

～

Planting Guide: page 20
Border Plan: page 21

Planting Guide (see pages 18–19)

1. *Chamaecyparis pisifera* 'Filifera Aurea' (golden Sawara cypress), H: 6 m (20 ft), S: 3 m (10 ft) after 20 years and, ultimately, H: 12 m (40 ft), S: 5 m (15 ft).

2. *E. fortunei* 'Silver Queen', H: 2.5 m (8 ft), S: 1.5 m (5 ft)

3. 3 x *Salvia officinalis* 'Purpurascens' (purple sage), H: 60 cm (2 ft), S: 90 cm (3 ft).

4. 3 x *Salvia officinalis* (sage), H: 60 cm (2 ft), S: 90 cm (3 ft).

5. 3 x *Festuca glauca* (blue fescue), H: 15 cm (6 in), S: 20 cm (8 in).

6. *Spiraea japonica* 'Goldflame', H and S: 75 cm (30 in).

7. *Berberis thunbergii* 'Atropurpurea Nana',

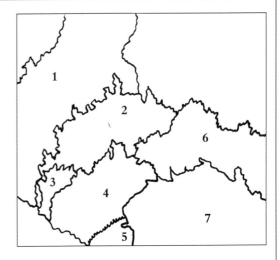

Plot size: length 3.5 m (12 ft); depth 1.8 m (6 ft)
H and S: 60 cm (2 ft).

little harm. If you are simply busy doing other things and choose not to be a slave to your garden, it will be possible to relax in a retreat of soft greens without that awful nagging urge to get up and pull out weeds, sow the next row of lettuce or deadhead the roses. There is a lot to recommend itself to borders of low-maintenance shrubs.

The key to successful plantings is to create a lively mixture of evergreen and deciduous shrubs, offering a pattern of different leaf colours and textures throughout the year. Your shrubs may not deliver a riot of summer colour, but will still look superb during winter when other gardens may suffer from lack of structure. For those who do not object to a little extra work, it is possible to leave empty pockets here and there where bedding plants can be used for occasional bursts of colour. *Pelargonium* species for

sunny positions or *Impatiens* for shady ones will perform in summer, while winter-flowering pansies or wallflowers plus clumps of daffodils and tulips will keep the display going through autumn, winter and spring.

For reliable winter effect, only one in three plants should be deciduous. As most of these will be of interest only during summer, make full use of any coloured-leaved varieties available. It is possible to have several *Philadelphus* (mock orange) not only for their scented flowers in early summer, but also for the various colours of their leaves. I am fond of *P.* 'Manteau d'Hermine' which has plain green leaves and scented, double, creamy white flowers and makes a spreading bush only 75 cm (30 in) high. *P. coronarius* 'Aureus' bears striking, gold leaves in spring, which gradually turn lime green in summer on a shrub eventually reaching a height of 2.5 m (8 ft) and a spread of 1.5 m (5 ft). Both this and *P. coronarius* 'Variegatus', which has handsome white-edged leaves, bear superbly fragrant flowers.

Shrubs with variegated foliage are best used economically, surrounded with plain green, purple or gold. Planting too many variegated plants together can look muddled rather than attractive. Another deciduous genus with good leaf colours is *Weigela*. As well as plain-leaved sorts, there is purple-leaved *W. florida* 'Foliis Purpureis', height and spread 1.5 m (5 ft), against which the pink early-summer flowers contrast well. Low and spreading, it reaches about 90 cm (3 ft). For its white-edged leaves, *W. florida* 'Aureovariegata' is effective and reaches a height and spread of 1.5 m (5 ft).

Larger, but excellent for their foliage, are some of the elders. I particularly like *Sambucus nigra* 'Guincho Purple', which can reach a height and spread of 4.5 m (15 ft). Flat heads of pink-tinged, white flowers open from pink buds which look superb against the dark purple foliage. Another good performer is a golden elder, *S. racemosa* 'Plumosa Aurea' which will grow to 3 m (10 ft) and bears deeply cut, golden leaves.

Evergreens with shiny, green leaves are good value, including the many different varieties of holly. A very lovely shrub is *Osmanthus delavayi*, which will grow slowly to a bush of 3 m (10 ft). Its neat, dark green leaves make an excellent foil for other colours and are joined by fragrant white flowers in spring. For a sheltered site, I would recommend an unusual shrub, *Drimys lanceolata* (syn. *D. aromatica*), often called the mountain pepper. This thrives in my garden, positioned in a semi-shaded spot facing north west. Deep red stems are complemented by shiny, pleasantly aromatic, oblong leaves, which are red when young, turning green. Small, star-shaped, white flowers make a good show in spring. Mature plants are said to reach a height of 3.5 m (12 ft), but mine has managed only 1.2 m (4 ft) in six years.

Bronze-purple evergreens can strike a deep note in a shrub border and are best represented by *Pittosporum tenuifolium* 'Tom Thumb'. Reaching a height and spread of only 75 cm (30 in), it is among the hardiest of its tribe. New spring shoots are green, but turn a lovely bronze as they mature. For a soft effect, the conifer *Cryptomeria japonica* 'Elegans' bears blue-green needles which create a silvery haze in summer, but turn bronze during winter. It reaches a height of 4.5 m (15 ft) but there is a dwarf form, *C. japonica* 'Elegans Compacta', which remains a smaller 90 cm (3 ft).

The Low-maintenance Shrub Border Plan

Low-maintenance plantings, such as that pictured on pages 18–19, are as much about reliability as effectiveness, and while this lovely combination of colourful leaves looks attractive, it is composed of shrubs which are hardy and well-tempered.

These plants will flourish in any good, well-drained soil and, apart from sage,

will withstand short periods of waterlogging in winter. They will thrive in full sun, collectively suiting all but a north-facing aspect.

If you have a narrower border, omit the *Chamaecyparis* and use the other plants set out in more of a straight line, yet staggered to make an informal pattern. There should be little maintenance, other than gently cutting back stems of any shrub which threatens to swamp others (at any time of year). Sages are short lived and may need replacing after three to five years.

I feel that borders planted solely with conifers can appear rather bulky and tedious, yet their definite shapes and reliable year-round presence are valuable in a shrub border. On page 18 the elegant golden cypress makes a beautiful addition to other shrubs which light up the backdrop of rather dour plantings. Depth is added by the bronze-purple tones of the purple-leaved sage and *Berberis*.

Spiraea japonica 'Goldflame' is a good subject for brightening up borders with its shrimp-pink, new, spring growth. This eventually yellows with age and is joined by heads of small, dense, pink flowers in summer. Both the spiraea and berberis are deciduous, leaving behind a complicated tracery of stems for the winter,

Where there have to be hard surfaces such as paths and drives, gardens can still be effectively planned using simple shapes. Here, clipped box contrasts beautifully with a late show of informal pink hydrangeas and hardy fuchsias.

∼

which can be enjoyed against the enduring foliage of the evergreens. Sages are small, evergreen shrubs, but can look a little bedraggled towards the tail end of winter. The trick is to prune back hard in spring, leaving behind short stumps of last year's stems from which new growth will burst forth, regenerating the plants. Their leaves can be used for cooking, just as if they were growing in a herb garden.

Colourful Evergreens

Among gold-leaved evergreens, *Choisya* 'Sundance' is hard to beat for its ability to light up a dull corner or augment an already interesting mixture of colours. The foliage on this Mexican orange is a little tender and should be protected from the freezing and drying effects of cold winter wind in exposed positions. It will also benefit from gentle shading from hot, scorching sun. Other than that, it is an easy plant to grow, reaching, usually, around 1.2-1.5 m (4-5 ft) but capable of 2.5 m (8 ft) in favourable conditions. If a plant should suffer blemishes or die back, you can easily restore it by pruning out damaged growth in spring. The scented, white flowers which open in early summer are pretty, but do not stand out as well as those on the plain green-leaved *C. ternata*.

Another easy golden evergreen is *Lonicera nitida* 'Baggesen's Gold', which makes a dense bush of neat, narrow leaves, reaching a height and spread of some 1.5 m (5 ft). An evergreen honeysuckle, it bears no resemblance to the fragrant climbers we usually associate with that name. There is a silvery version, *L. n.* 'Silver Beauty', which is similar, with a silvery-white edge to the leaf that lends it a light, ethereal appeal.

If silver is required in a border, then *Senecio* is a wise choice. Tough and easy going, *S. greyi* (now correctly *Brachyglottis greyi*) reaches a height of 1-1.2 m (3-4 ft) and spread of 1.2-1.8 m (4-6 ft) and produces oval leaves felted with dense, grey-white hairs on top and ghostly white beneath. Yellow, daisy-like flowers are produced in summer, but are not a significant part of the attraction. I rather like *S. greyi* 'Drysdale', which has a neat, wavy edge to the leaves.

Formality

Shrubs can also be used to make strong, formal shapes in a low-maintenance garden. This relies on careful planning and involves a small amount of regular maintenance. The narrow border that forms a boundary to my front garden is dominated by a wayward dog rose hedge which is tough and looks after itself apart from a tidy-up in summer and a more thorough pruning in spring, when some older, taller pieces are cut back to encourage new growth. To smarten this up, there is a large box ball at one end and a tall, cube-shaped yew with outward-sloping sides at the other end. The box is clipped twice and the yew once during the summer. A dense undergrowth of yellow-flowered, fern-leaved *Corydalis lutea*, with a height and spread of 20-30 cm (8-12 in), comes up every spring at the foot of the hedge. Then what would traditionally have been lawn is now a drive of smart, brownish-pink chippings which makes a hard standing for two cars either side of a *Magnolia soulangiana*, with a height and spread of 6 m (20 ft). Even in small spaces, it is possible to soften a hard surface by retaining as much greenery as possible.

Front gardens have to accommodate drives and paths, and a formal mix of clipped shapes and hard surfaces is effective and easy to maintain. I know a front garden which by necessity is a hard, crazy-paved area, but reaching up out of circular beds are amazing topiary shapes, trained in yew, of linked circles in the shapes of mice and other figures.

Both box and yew respond to hard pruning, and if they gradually become too large or misshapen, they can be cut back into other shapes. I am hoping to reduce my box shape to a much smaller ball. Spring is the best time to carry out this ruthless treatment, when the plants are naturally making new growth.

Mixed Low-maintenance Borders

~

At first glance it may seem that attempting to create a delightful mixture of plants in a border which requires little maintenance is like trying to have your cake and eat it too. Yet there is a modern trend towards a style of planting which, though evolved for much larger landscapes, can be scaled down effectively for ordinary gardens.

A tapestry of colourful foliage with a few seasonal flowers can be enjoyed without too much effort by planting a mixture of low-maintenance shrubs, a subject discussed at length in the preceding chapter. However, if a gardener wishes to create a border of lovely flowers, while at the same time cutting back on work, more thought is required. Ordinary mixed borders usually contain a framework of shrubs, with perhaps a small tree for height, plus herbaceous perennials, bulbs and annuals arranged together for good year-round impact. Most are labour intensive, involving much weeding, replanting, staking and tying, watering and feeding.

The trick is to select a range of plants which blend together beautifully, give some interest in every season, suit the soil and aspect and grow well in harmony with each other. For this planting to be truly low-maintenance, the gardener has to take a deep breath and a couple of steps back. If some plants begin to suffer and show signs of being swamped by others, to an extent this has to be allowed. As long as enough of the plant choices were right, those which suit the spot best will take over and thrive.

The philosophy of this planting style is said to originate, like many other things, from the USA where it is hailed as the New American Style. Such blendings of reliable herbaceous perennials and grasses have also been widely embraced by German landscape designers, who in many areas are unable by law to use chemical pesticides and weedkillers in their public places. As a result, they have moved away from the high-maintenance bedding schemes still widely used in British public gardens, and settled for a more environmentally sensitive, softer mix of plants. The effect is certainly different, but very pleasant.

Although hailed as new and revolutionary (which it may well be to public spaces), many individual gardeners in Britain have been exercising their common sense for many years. As a result, examples of this mixed, low-maintenance planting can be seen in private gardens the length and breadth of the country. It is a simple format, falling back on knowledge of soil, climate and the individual vagaries of any garden. To understand a plot thoroughly, you have to watch it carefully through an entire year. Look out for borders where frost hardly ever penetrates and others where plants

This impressive and colourful combination of plants looks good, will largely take care of itself and is smartly set of by a mulch of gravel along an attractive path.

~

Planting Guide: page 27
Border Plan: page 28

are liable to be frozen on a regular basis. Some areas are baked dry and roots from nearby hedges or trees may suck the life out of a border, making the soil poor and impoverished. Other beds may be prone to a high water table and be constantly waterlogged or, worse, be prone to a fluctuating water table. Look out for nicely sheltered spots and also those

Planting Guide (see page 26)

1. *Rosa* 'Albéric Barbier', H: 1.5 m (5 ft), S: 1.2 m (4 ft).

2. *Salvia officinalis* 'Icterina' (variegated sage), H: 60 cm (2 ft), S: 90 cm (3 ft).

3. 2 x *Armeria maritima* (thrift), H and S: 15 cm (6 in).

4. *Spiraea japonica* 'Little Princess'. H: 45 cm (18 in) S: 90 cm (3 ft)

5. *Alchemilla mollis* (lady's mantle), H and S: 45 cm (18 in).

6. 3 x *Centranthus ruber* (red valerian), H: 60–90 cm (2–3 ft), S: 60 cm (2 ft).

7. Fresh green, deciduous shrub such as *Spiraea douglasii*, H and S: 1.8 m (6 ft).

8. Small, purple-leaved shrub such as *Salvia offic inalis* 'Purpurascens' (purple sage), H: 60 cm (2 ft), S: 90 cm (3 ft).

9. Climbing plant such as clematis or climbing rose.

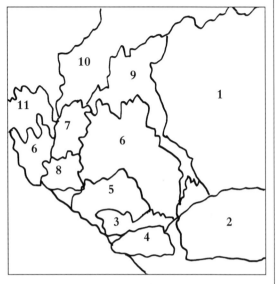

Plot size: length 3.5 m (12 ft); depth 1.8 m (6 ft)

10. Honeysuckle such as *Lonicera periclymenum* 'Belgica' (early Dutch honeysuckle) H and S: 3.6 m (12 ft)

11. *Rosmarinus officinalis* (rosemary) H and S: 1.5 m (5 ft)

which are whipped by the wind. A knowledgeable gardener, or even a novice armed with a good book and an enquiring mind, should be able to match plants with positions to give the right combination to succeed in any border. The ultimate secret is to work *with* prevailing conditions and not against them.

Summer displays in sunny borders rely upon herbaceous perennials for their flower colour. Groups of tough stalwarts like *Rudbeckia* 'Goldsturm', with a height of 75 cm (30 in) and a spread of 30 cm (1 ft) or more, and *Echinacea purpurea*, height 90 cm (3 ft) and spread 50 cm (20 in), – known as cone flowers because

of the dome of disc florets in the middle of each flower – mixed with *Kniphofia* 'Royal Standard' (red hot pokers), height 1.2 m (4 ft) and spread 60 cm (2 ft), grow with grasses, which look good right into autumn. Shrubs take over for winter, with showy leaves, stems or winter flowers, then the display of flowers begins again with spring bulbs as the perennials grow afresh.

Maintenance is kept to a minimum because less is expected of the plants than if they were being grown and gardened in the conventional sense. As long as plants are established in a moist autumn or spring, they should not require additional watering. Feeding should be kept to an absolute minimum (if given at all) and all that tedious lifting, dividing and replanting which we are urged to do every few years should be ignored until absolutely necessary. Enriching the soil with copious quantities of well-rotted manure or compost goes against the theory, since this will only cause the plants to grow taller and sappier, making them less drought-tolerant and more in need of support. All that is really being suggested is that plants are allowed to grow more as they do in the wild.

The Low-maintenance Border Plan

The plants in the border shown on page 26 require a well-drained soil which is not too rich. There should be a happy medium between the needs of centranthus and armeria for a rather poor soil and the rose for a more fertile spot, though 'Albéric Barbier' can tolerate poorer soils than some. This selection will need full sun to thrive and can be scaled up or down to suit any border. Without the backing of roses and shrubs, the front plants could be used to fill a narrow strip of soil along a wall or fence.

It is undoubtedly the balance of purple and red that contributes to the success of this low-maintenance border. The old-fashioned rambling rose has superb, deep green foliage and a multitude of flowers which, combined, have the effect of bending the branches down with their weight. The creamy-white, moderately fragrant blooms look almost butter-yellow in bud and appear mainly in summer but with a speckling of blooms into autumn. Roses, once established, send down deep, woody roots well able to tolerate drought, as can the red valerian. This doughty plant can often be seen growing in stone walls with catmint, their roots hardly clinging to any soil at all. *Alchemilla,* sage and thrift are equally drought-tolerant and need no staking.

Sometimes, the spaces in a garden are as important as the structure of the planting. This is illustrated well here where an eye for shapes has stilled the hand when it came to planting. Instead of more plants being crammed in, they have space to stand out, the gaps being filled with a mulch of moisture-retaining, weed-suppressing gravel which matches the path. Maintenance will only really consist of curbing the spread of valerian and *Spiraea* and trimming back the sages in spring.

Trial and Error

After struggling to settle totally unsuitable plants into the uninvitingly poor, sandy soil of my own garden, there was only one course of action. This was to rethink my planting ideas and apply a common-sense approach to the west-facing border in my front garden. There is no room here for the loose drifts of herbaceous perennials proposed for larger municipal schemes, but plants can be settled in groups of three, five or seven and left to see which thrive. Because the border is small, I concentrated on plants which would flower for long periods.

One year on, a group of moisture-loving *Geum rivale* have died off, but their space is colonized by a thriving clump of spreading *Phygelius capensis* (Cape figwort), with its stems up to 1.2 m (4 ft) long, bearing bright orange flowers. Coming from the other direction is a large grouping of seed-grown lavender. The *Carpenteria californica* at the back offers evergreen shape and is kept to 90 cm (3 ft) by pruning, so it can be sheltered by a low wall. Its large, white flowers are a bonus in early summer. Perennials like aromatic, seed-grown *Agastache* (anise), with a height of 90 cm (3 ft) and spread of 30 cm (1 ft), and white-flowered *Campanula takesimana* are quite good at supporting themselves, but have the advantage of being able to lean on a living support system.

Although willows are associated with moist soils, my *Salix alba vitellina* 'Britzensis', height 1.5 m (5 ft) and spread 1 m (3 ft) with pruning, seem to love the hot, dry situation and, from a hard cutting back every March, send up slender stems which support the perennials running through them. In winter, when the perennials have died down and the willow leaves fallen, their stems glow a beautiful orange in the weak sun.

Their display is augmented by the needles of low-growing, dwarf pines and silvery, carpeting leaves of *Veronica incana* (from seed) which reaches no more than 15 cm (6 in) in height with a spread of 30 cm (1 ft). In summer the scene bursts to life with the yellow-red flowers of *Gaillardia grandiflora* and yellow daisies of *Anthemis tinctoria* 'E.C. Buxton', as well as

unusual, seed-grown *Helenium hoopesii* which comes from the Rocky Mountains and achieves a height of 38 cm (15 in) and a spread of 45 cm (18 in). Ground-cover *Rosa* 'Suffolk', which grows to just 60 cm (2 ft) high with a spread of 90 cm (3 ft) and bears not just neat, red flowers but pretty, orange hips too, thrives well, as does *Crocosmia* 'Planchon', which reaches a height of 60 cm (2 ft) and a spread of 23 cm (9 in). Rising up to flower late in the autumn, is an unusual Michaelmas daisy called *Aster turbinellus*, height 1.2 m (4 ft) and spread 60 cm (2 ft). Its haze of tiny, purple-blue flowers opens effectively on wiry stems. During a summer of drought, none of these plants was watered and they were barely fed. This kept their growth to a minimum, avoiding wilting, sappy stems prone to disease and in need of time-consuming staking.

Once the main plants in such a bed are established, there is the opportunity for a keen gardener to add more. Smaller plants can be used as interplanting, so that their colours weave in amongst the others, tying the whole scheme together. Look for plants which hold their foliage close to the ground and send up a thin, unobtrusive stem of flowers. Such plants rarely need staking and do not produce masses of foliage at middle height which might flop about and get in the way of existing plants. This makes *Allium* species (ornamental onions) excellent for the job. Their bulbs can be planted between other plants during autumn and their slender stems push through existing growth to hold rounded flower heads of various sizes. Individual flowers are star-shaped and purple in colour and, while they open mostly during early summer, they die gracefully and the dried, papery heads are still around by autumn. Seeds are scattered about and will germinate, spreading these plants throughout borders in a very pleasant way. Their gentle colours blend well with most plants, especially lavenders and other plants with silvery foliage.

Other examples include purple fennel, whose feathery leaves rise to about 1–1.2 m (3–4 ft) effectively among other plants. Giant hybrid thrifts which can be raised easily from seed make strong clumps of low, linear leaves from which drumsticks of tightly packed, pink flowers rise up mostly during spring and early summer, but can appear at virtually any time of the year. These can be dotted and threaded between other plants and show reasonable tolerance to drought. *Gaura lindheimeri*, a perennial related to rose bay willow herb, is effective too. Airy, pink flowers are borne on long, slender, waving stems and, though capable of making large plants, they mix well with others.

Traditional Low-maintenance Ground Cover

I have found the relaxed method of low-maintenance gardening (described above) both satisfying and exciting. However, for gardeners who prefer a bit more order in their borders, there is the option of creating satisfying arrangements using mixed low-maintenance plants which knit together to form a weed-suppressing mass. A mixture of shrubs and perennials,

they can be effective as well as beautiful.

The method consists of choosing an interesting mixture of trees and shrubs, then infilling with good ground-covering plants. Think carefully about whether evergreen or deciduous ground cover is needed and check before planting. Early maintenance consists of weeding between the plants as they grow, then later making sure that groupings, such as spurges, ivy and *Vinca* (periwinkle) are not too successful and in danger of smothering the larger plants they are supposed to set off.

One of the best types is hardy geraniums. Planted in groups of three or five, they quickly spread, and as there are many interesting sorts, they are very collectable. Among the best weed suppressors is semi-evergreen *G. macrorrhizum*, which reaches some 30 cm (1 ft) tall and produces magenta flowers in early summer. The aromatic leaves are a good, solid shape and turn orange-red in autumn. Another of my favourites is *G. renardii,* whose rounded, lobed, soft green leaves are superb. It, too, reaches up to 30 cm (1 ft) and its flowers, borne in early summer, are white with dark veins. The whole plant dies back for winter.

One of the most exciting geraniums is *G.* 'Ann Folkard', height 50 cm (20 in) and spread 90 cm (3 ft), whose stems are almost climbing. Tuck plants in amongst other ground coverers and it will grow over and through them without swamping. Rich magenta flowers are produced right through summer and autumn, making an ideal complement to leaves which are a bright, yellowish green. I have used mine in a shady bed along a

north wall, where it flounces over the glossy, kidney-shaped leaves of low-growing *Asarum europeum*, itself a lovely ground-cover evergreen for shade. It then clambers over small, winter-flowering *Rhododendron* 'Olive', brightening up an area which would otherwise be devoid of flowers all summer.

Good evergreen ground-cover plants

A conventional mixture of spreading plants will knit together to make a fine weed-suppressing ground cover. Here, Hebe speciosa *flowers next door to the large leaves of moisture-loving* Ligularia *'Desdemona' which contrast well with the bright green, spiky-shaped foliage of* Iris sibirica *and pink spikes of* Persicaria affine.

~

31

for shady spots are the dead nettles. I like the more compact sorts, especially *Lamium maculatum* 'Pink Nancy', with a height of 15 cm (6 in) and a spread of 90 cm (3 ft). Its neat leaves are heavily marked with white, making it stand out well in a gloomy place. Pink flowers, borne in late spring and early summer, make warm spots of colour against the foliage. An unusual choice for shade would be *Luzula nivea,* height 45 cm (1 1/2 ft) and spread 45–60 cm (18–24 in), the low-growing snowy woodrush. This ever-green perennial, which makes a tuft of typical, rush-like leaves edged with white hairs, bears white flowers held above the foliage in early summer. It can thrive in dry shade – grow it from seed if a large group is required.

Grasses make effective ground cover and there are plenty of both evergreen and deciduous choices. An idea I am about to try in my own garden involves plantings of evergreen *Agrostis canina* 'Silver Needles', a dwarf, soft-textured grass with bright, silvery-white leaves with a narrow, green stripe. From a distance, plants appear ghostly white and produce typical, plume-like grass flowers in summer. It is best to enjoy these briefly, then clip them off so that the foliage does not deteriorate. Against these, the grass-like lily-relative

Ophiopogon planiscapus 'Nigrescens', height 23 cm (9 in) and spread 30 cm (1ft), will give a complete contrast with its tufts of almost black leaves. Given time, *Ophiopogon* spreads into suckering clumps which hold their own against most weeds. The new introduction *Festuca glauca* 'Golden Toupee', height and spread 10 cm (4 in), is another soft-leaved, dwarf grass which makes hum-mocks of slender, golden foliage matched almost exactly by the colour of summer flowers. This associates well with *F. glauca*. If you can, track down *F. glauca* 'Elijah Blue', which is a more intense blue colour.

For more conventional planting, mass together reliable subjects like shade- tol-erant *Euphorbia amygdalpides robbiae,* an evergreen sub-shrub known as Mrs. Robb's bonnet, which rises to 45–60 cm (18–24 in) tall and bears glossy, leathery leaves joined by greenish-yellow flowers from February to April. As with all euphorbias, take care as the sap is poiso-nous and can irritate sensitive skin. *Persicaria bistorta* 'Superba' (syn. *Polygonum bistorta* 'Superbum'), with a height of 60–75 cm (2–2½ ft) and a spread of 60 cm (2 ft), is a sun- or shade-lover excellent for its weed-proof spread of roots, semi-ever-green foliage and spikes of pink flowers all summer long.

Seasonal Borders

~

There is a temptation, in today's smaller garden, to plant every border with structural shrubs and labour-saving ground cover. This multi-seasonal approach may look tidy all year and satisfy the need for low-maintenance, but it lacks those crescendos of colour which make gardening such a satisfying pastime. When a gardener's plans come right, borders can flare into a succession of sensational displays. Even damp, cold winters can be enlivened by sections of border planted to deliver welcome, scented blooms, and colour in foliage, stems and bark. One of the benefits of gardening in the British climate is the changing seasons and the challenge of making the best of them.

SPRING

The first signs of spring are eagerly awaited in that long drag of January and February after the flurry and excitement of Christmas. In a well-planted garden, sightings of yellow *Eranthis hyemalis* (winter aconites), height 5–10 cm (2–4 in) and spread 8–10 cm (3–4 in), nestled in their green collars, *Galanthus* (snowdrops), and species crocus can come as early as January, raising spirits and making spring seem that little bit closer.

Clusters of spring bulbs can easily be slipped into any border, but an entire area given over to spring plantings needs more consideration. In a small garden, the best place for them is often in a semi-wild area created around a tree. Trends in garden design may come and go, but the traditional idea of enjoying formality by the house and an increasing wildness as you move away from it, not only translates well to small, modern gardens, but makes sense too. In restricted spaces, the best site for a tree is usually towards the bottom of a garden. Here it is unlikely to shade the house, fallen leaves are not so much of a nuisance, and potentially troublesome roots are unlikely to penetrate foundations.

Borders under and around deciduous trees can be a challenge to plant successfully, yet are ideal places in which to create spring gardens. Choose a couple of seasonal shrubs to add structure, then bring together a mass of flowering bulbs and perennials. Most of these will have completed their display by the time leaves appear on the tree, creating a shady canopy for the rest of the summer. Such a border can be a joy, threaded with narrow paths or stepping stones, all the better from which to admire delicate blooms. Another excellent position for a spring garden is in the narrow, often shady borders to be found along the feet of a pergola. Spring beauties can finish their display before the pergola is burdened with the foliage and flowers of roses, honeysuckle and clematis.

In the shade of a birch tree, this border has become home for a lovely collection of mid-spring plants.

〜

Planting Guide: page 35
Border Plan: below

The Spring Border Plan

This border, shown in the photograph above, is essentially a woodland planting and the formula for success involves a soil which manages to be both light and moist yet freely derained and not prone to waterlogging. On both clay and sandy soils, the addition of copious quantities of leaf mould will help build the right texture. When first preparing clay soil for this sort of planting, dig deeply and incorporate plenty of coarse grit to improve drainage.

By its very nature, a woodland border is usually in semi-shade. Light is able to penetrate the tree canopies during late winter and spring, enabling a wide range of early-flowering bulbs and perennials to grow. Later, leaves cause more dense shade and the plants that take over need to be more tolerant of this.

Planting Guide (see page 34)

1. 20 x *Ranunculus ficaria* (celandine) and 40 x *Galanthus* (snowdrop) – buy 'in the green' in spring.

2. *Primula*, H and S: 15–20 cm (6–8in).

3. 5 x *Narcissus* (choose a medium-sized type 20–25 cm (8–10 in) tall.

4. 4 x *Digitalis purpurea* (foxglove), H: 1–1.5 m (3–5 ft), S: 30 cm (1 ft).

5. 10 x *Muscari* (grape hyacinth), H: 15–20 cm (6–8 in), S: 8–10 cm (3–4 in).

6. 20 x *Fritillaria verticillata*, H: 90 cm (3 ft), S: 10 cm (4 in).

7. 3 x *Nectaroscordium siculum*, H: 1.2 m (4 ft), S: 30–45 cm (12–18 in).

8. 6 x *Pulmonaria* (lungwort), H: 30 cm (1 ft), S: 30–45 cm (12–18 in).

9. 7 x *Colchicum* (foliage).

10. *Betula pendula* (silver birch), H: 6–9 m (20–30 ft), S: 2.5–3.5 m (8–12 ft) in 20 years.

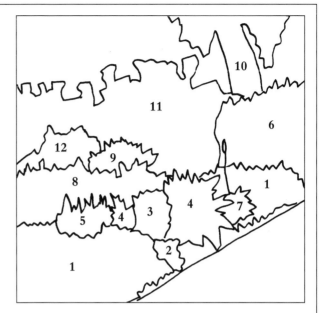

Plot size: length 3.5 m(12 ft); depth 2.5 m (8 ft)

11. 20 x *Fritillaria imperialis* (crown imperial), yellow (F. i 'Maxima lutea) and orange-red varieties, H: 1–1.5 m (3–5 ft), S: 23–30 cm (9–12 in).

12. 3 x *Myrrhis odorata* (sweet Cicely), H and S: 60 cm (2 ft).

Although this is quite a deep bed, the idea can easily be copied in more restricted areas by using fewer plants in each group.

Birch trees are ideal for smaller gardens, because they tend to be quite narrow and their small leaves cast less shade than some others. Alternatives to the common silver birch could include two of my favourites. *Betula utilis* 'Jaquemontii', height 15 m (50 ft) and spread 7.5 m (25 ft), is well known for its stunning white trunk and *B. ermanii*, height 15 m (50 ft) and spread 7.5 m (25 ft), for its peeling pink bark. If you want large shrubs or trees which will flower in spring above the other plants, choose one of the spring- flowering *Viburnums*, a *Magnolia* (check the eventual height and spread of the variety you choose) or an ornamental cherry tree.

I can remember the first time I saw a bulb of *Fritillaria imperialis* (crown imperial), height up to 1.5 m (5 ft) and spread 23–30 cm (9–12 in), when I was a teenager working in a pet and garden store on Saturdays. I took one home in lieu of some of my wages and planted it in the stony soil of my parents' south-east London garden. It has now grown into a clump and has bloomed, year after year ever since. They are remarkably showy and make bold focal points in spring borders. *F. verticillata,* height up to 90 cm (3 ft) and spread 8–10cm (3–4 in), is far daintier in appearance, forming a cloud of white flowers. *Fritillaria* bulbs should be planted in autumn, 10–15 cm (4–6 in) deep for most kinds, but 20 cm (8 in) for the crown imperial. The bulbs thrive only in well-drained soil, so where soils are naturally clay-like with a tendency towards waterlogging, it is even more important to condition the soil well and incorporate grit over a large area.

In a smaller garden, it would be as well to add a couple of shrubs and some summer-flowering, shade-tolerant herbaceous perennials, to ensure that this pretty border remains interesting. (On an acid soil, evergreen *Pieris japonica,* height and spread 2.5 m (8 ft), would be lovely with its sprays of white flowers in May and bronze-red new shoots.) *Cornus alba* 'Elegantissima', height and spread 3 m (10 ft), will provide red stems in winter, as well as variegated foliage during summer.

Helleborus orientalis (Lenten rose), height and spread 45 cm (18 in), makes a lovely addition to a spring scene, and is most effective when used in bold drifts. It is a good idea to cut away the old foliage at the end of winter, to make a clear path for stems of flowers and the new leaves when they come. Apart from the green tufts of foliage which accompany bulbs, spring foliage is not always exciting, which is why marbled *Arum italicum* 'Marmoratum', whose leaves start growing in autumn and stay through winter to spring, is so valuable. This reaches a height of 12–25 cm (5–10 in) depending on soil moisture and richness. Just remember to remove its poisonous berries in summer if there are children in the garden.

Spring Plants for Shade

In an otherwise sunny garden, I have a shaded, north-facing border along by a garage wall. A slightly raised, semi-circular bed has made an ideal home for a predominantly spring garden. In order for woodland plants, particularly those that prefer a slightly acid soil, to flourish, I have added lots of leaf mould to the soil. This humus-rich, well-drained yet sufficiently moisture-retentive soil is ideal for plants that grow naturally under trees. The addition will benefit any soil, whether it be thin and poor or sticky and clay-like. While some spring-flowering plants are not especially fussy about soil, others, mostly the finer kinds like North American trilliums, will fare far better if properly catered for.

Against the wall I have planted *Camellia japonica* 'Alba Plena', height 4 m (13 ft) and spread 1.8 m (6 ft) with pruning, for its neat, pure-white, double flowers. Camellias really are the prima donnas of the spring garden. All too often we wait for plants to establish, water them faithfully from mid to late summer to be sure of a good set of buds, then watch helplessly as frost scorches the petals as they open. It pays to stand by with horticultural fleece or old net curtains, to cover vulnerable buds and flowers on freezing nights. For an understated garden, I would opt for the neater-flowered varieties like mine, in colours of pink, red or white, though I know many love the more opulent blossoms of hybrids such as 'Debbie' and 'Donation' which have huge, frilly, pink blooms.

Next to this, on the wall, is a plant that every owner of a north-facing wall should have. *Chaenomeles speciosa* 'Moerloosei', height 2.5 m (8 ft) and spread 2.7 m (9 ft) with pruning, is a member of that group of plants loosely referred to as Japanese quinces or just 'japonicas'. This one lends itself beautifully to being trained in a fan shape against a wall and opens its apple blossom-coloured flowers during February and March. Simply tie in stems to fill gaps and cut away surplus side shoots to about 12 cm (5 in) after flowering.

Under these, the dwarf bulb *Scilla mischtschenkoana* has naturalized to make a carpet of pale blue, flowering close to the ground at first, then reaching, individually, some 10 cm (4 in) in height and 5 cm (2 in) in spread. In front of these are planted two early-flowering rhododendrons. *R.* 'Olive' is superb, with clear pink flowers which open in January and last for at least six weeks, and *R. dauricum* 'Hokkaido' is a dainty white. Both only reach about 1.5 m (5 ft) in height and spread. Later on, in May, the unusual x *Ledodendron* 'Arctic Tern', which makes a compact bush 90 cm (3 ft) high, opens its heads of small, white flowers. In April, the really lovely woodland flowers like *Trillium sessile*, height 30–38 cm (12–15 in) and spread 30–45 cm (12–18 in), *T. grandiflorum*, height 38 cm (15 in) and spread 30 cm

(1 ft), and *Sanguinaria canadensis* 'Flore Pleno', height 10–15 cm (4–6 in) and spread 30 cm (1 ft) can bloom in the spaces, before hardy ferns, pulmonarias and others crowd them out.

EARLY SUMMER

Many gardens, including mine, reach a peak at the beginning of the summer season, when summer growth is still in its first flush and the soil moist from spring rain. Early summer weather is generally fine and the garden full of promising buds. Many deciduous shrubs and climbers bloom at this time, filling the air with the perfume of honeysuckle and mock orange.

Roses open their flowers in great profusion too, with almost every type at its best towards the end of June. This includes the old-fashioned roses, many of which will flower only once. Even repeat-flowering kinds like many hybrid teas and floribundas never quite reach that same combination of flower and freshness. Their full, often scented blooms combine beautifully with early-flowering herbaceous perennials like *Delphinium*, *Hesperis matrionalis* (sweet rocket), with a height of 75 cm (2 ft 6 in) and spread of 60 cm (2 ft), *Aquilegia* and *Stachys macrantha* (betony), with a height and spread of 30 cm (1 ft).

Walls and fences behind borders can also come alive at this time of year, because many of the showiest climbers flower during early summer. Queen among these must surely be wisteria, though it can drive some gardeners mad

Planting Guide (see page 38)

1. *Chamaecyparis lawsoniana* 'Stewartii' (Lawson's cypress), H: 9 m (30 ft), S: 2.5 m (8 ft) after 20 years, but ultimately H: 15 m (50 ft), S: 4 m (12 ft).

2. 2 x *Cornus alba* 'Aurea', H: 1–1.2 m (3–4 ft), S: 90 cm (3 ft) if stooled annually.

3. *Caryopteris* x *clandonensis*, H and S: 90 cm (3 ft).

4. 3 x *Achillea* 'Moonshine', H: 60 cm (2 ft), S: 50 cm (20 in).

5. 9 (3 groups of 3) x *Felicia amelloides* (king fisher daisy), H: 23 cm (9 in), S: 30 cm (1 ft).

6. 3 x *Lilium regale* (regal lily), H: 60–120 cm (2–4 ft), S: 30 cm (1 ft).

7. 3 x *Iris* (foliage), H: 60 cm (2 ft), S: 15 cm (6 in).

8. *Potentilla fruticosa* variety, H: 60 cm (2 ft), S: 90 cm (3 ft).

9. 3 x *Hosta* such as 'Honeybells', H: 60 cm (2 ft), S: 90 cm (3 ft).

10. Hardy *Geranium*, H and S: 45 cm (18 in).

11. *Lavandula angustifolia* 'Hidcote', H and S: 60 cm (2 ft).

12. *Argyranthemum* 'Jamaica Primrose' (marguerite), H and S: 90 cm (3 ft).

13. *Osteospermum* 'Buttermilk', H: 60 cm (2 ft), S: 30 cm (1 ft).

14. 3 x *Delphinium*, H: 1.2–1.8 m (4–6 ft), S: 1.2 m (4 ft).

15. *Viburnum rhytidophyllum*, H and S: 6 m (20 ft).

16. *Rosa* 'Wedding Day', H: 9 m (30 ft), S: 4.5 m (15 ft).

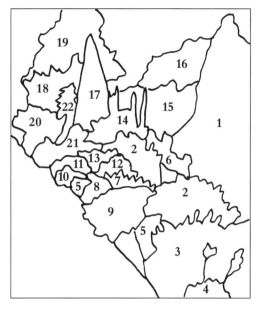

Plot size: length 9 m (30 ft); depth 2.75 m (9 ft)

17. *Chamaecyparis lawsoniana* 'Pottenii' (Lawson's cypress), H: 3 m (10 ft), S: 90 cm (3 ft) in 10 years, H: 7.5 m (25 ft), S: 1.5 m (5 ft) in 20 years, possibly 12 m (40 ft) high ultimately.

18. *Sambucus racemosa* 'Plumosa Aurea' (golden cut-leaved elder), H and S: 2.5–3 m (8–10 ft) if stooled.

19. *Robinia pseudoacacia* 'Frisia', H and S: 6 m (20 ft), S: 3 m (10 ft) in 20 years.

20. 3 x *Hemerocallis* (day lily), H and S: 90 cm (3 ft).

21. 2 x *Anemone* x *hybrida*, H: 1.2 m (4 ft), S: 60 cm (2 ft).

22. *Nicotiana sylvestris* (tobacco plant), H: 1.2 m (4 ft), S: 75 cm (30 in).

This is a fresh, early-summer border of classic style and distinction, using a good mixture of trees, shrubs, herbaceous perennials, bulbs and tender perennials.

Planting Guide: above
Border Plan: page 40

by taking many years to bloom. It is always a good plan to buy a reliable, named variety (such as *W. floribunda* 'Kuchi-beni', *W. f.* 'Peaches and Cream' or *W. sinensis* 'Prolific') which, after proper training, should take only three or four years to start flowering. I know some plants which are still not producing flowers after ten or even twelve years. Correct pruning by reducing laterals to 15 cm (6 in) during summer and cutting plants back hard to spurs containing just a couple of buds in winter helps keep excessive growth at bay and encourages maximum flowering. A more reliable flowerer in the same family as wisteria is *Robinia hispida* (rose acacia), height and spread 3 m (10 ft). This usually blooms from the first or second year of planting and carries on doing so faithfully, year after year. The leaflets are lovely too, being bright green ovals with small points, more like midrib extensions, at the tips.

Reliable plants for the fronts of borders are useful to know. *Veronica gentianoides,* height and spread 45 cm (18 in), makes a mat of leaves from which blue spikes of small, sky blue flowers rise up during May and June. Interspersed with *Alchemilla mollis* (lady's mantle), height and spread 50 cm (20 in), and *Sedum spectabile,* height and spread 45 cm (18 in), along the front of a border, it makes a strong edge. Although this veronica flowers only once, the other plants gradually take over, so that by the end of summer, the sedum is in full swing. This sort of repetitious planting works well along the margins of paths.

Another good edger is *Polemonium carneum,* a kind of Jacob's ladder. Reaching only 38 cm (15 in) in height and spread, it starts opening its clear pink flowers in May and finishes its first flush around July. Trim back the flower heads and it will be in bloom again by mid-August. To make several large patches cheaply, raise this delightful plant from seed.

The Early Summer Border Plan

A well-conditioned, loamy soil would suit all the plants shown in the border on page 38. The best way to ensure fertility is to apply a good mulch of well-rotted garden compost or manure in autumn or spring when the soil is moist. These plants would thrive in sun or semi-shade. This is a large border, but the idea could be scaled down if the back row of large shrubs, trees and conifers were removed. A similar assortment of plants could fill a 3.5 m (12 ft) by 1.8 m (6 ft) border if just one each of *Cornus, Hosta* and *Delphinium* were used.

Light greenish-yellow repeats itself throughout this border, with the addition, here and there, of blue, pink and orange. Although it is probably enjoying its peak in June, with the lilies, *delphinium* and rambling rose in full bloom, there is plenty of interest left for the rest of summer and winter. A border like this is ideal for a smaller garden, where, as one plant stops flowering, another will come on to replace it. Thus there is a gradual unfurling of interest until winter, when the attractive outlines of trees and evergreens remain.

If your neighbours have trees and shrubs, these can be made to look like the extending back of your border. Here the bright golden tones of the robinia and golden conifer give the border some form. In the middle, the evergreen *Viburnum rhytidophyllum* will gradually grow larger to take over as a main feature for the winter. *Leycesteria* is deciduous, but the bright green stems are decorative, as are the strings of purple bracts, small white flowers and berries that dangle in summer.

Golden cut-leaved elder is a plant of the early summer and it will grow large if not cut back really hard, almost to ground level, every spring. Feed and water it well during the summer to compensate for such rough treatment. Temporary plants like the *Argyranthemum* (marguerite) and *Felicia amelloides* (kingfisher daisy) will be removed at the end of summer and can be replaced with winter-flowering pansies or wallflowers for winter and spring. *Hemerocallis* (day lilies) are not particularly long-lasting in flower, but this voluptuous group of bold orange and red flowers will be followed, at the other end, by *Caryopteris* x *clandonensis* which will open its blue flowers in late summer.

Unless the soil is unusually moisture-retentive, it would be a good plan, when planting a border like this, to build in some sort of irrigation system. Automatic drippers, releasing water close to the ground, or a system of seep hoses, would keep the soil moist – and the plants happy – in the most efficient way possible.

LATE SUMMER

To keep borders interesting right through the summer and into autumn is important and challenging. When plans work, plantings can look almost as exciting at the close of summer as they did during the freshness of the early part. A late summer border can be as classy as the soft, billowing roses and harmonies of fresh, young foliage or flowers that come with the beginning of the season. Not only do plants have to be carefully chosen, but they often have to be nursed through droughts too. There is also room for some quirkiness in the late garden, when wonderful clashes of pink and orange, fruit and flower can be allowed to take place. It is, after all, the month when dahlias start to bloom and there has never been anything subtle about their flowers.

Plan a surprise for late summer by growing something a little out of the ordinary, capable of impressing garden visitors. One year I grew a mixture of gourds which we planted against my 2 m (7 ft) high back fence, which forms the backdrop to my dry shingle border. By September, after much nipping out of shoots and removal of excessive leaf, they had covered all the bare patches on the fence and were setting a collection of round, warty and bottle-shaped ornamental fruits. In the shingle beds is an expanding collection of *Salvias,* most of which come into flower towards the end of summer. The combination of brilliant blue, purple or red *Salvia* flowers with the large leaves and hilarious fruits of the gourds in the background made a

This classic border offers plenty of late summer interest, while managing to retain the freshness of its early summer counterpart.

~

Planting Guide: page 44
Border Plan: page 43

brilliant finale to summer.

There are several plants, stalwarts of the late scene, which demand a mention. Rudbeckias are invaluable, making masses of bright yellow or orange flowers with dark centres, shaped like large daisies.

Some, like R. 'Marmalade', are half-hardy annuals and will flower profusely from a spring sowing made under glass. Others, like R. 'Goldsturm' are perennial and therefore better value, as they will reappear year after year. Both are capable of reaching some 75 cm (30 in), though drought, which they tolerate well, will dwarf them. Neither needs staking.

Hardy fuchsias make worthy plants too, coming into their own as they combine with other late performers like blue-flowered *Caryopteris* x *clandonensis*, with a height and spread of 90 cm (3 ft). In most

Showing just how lovely late-summer flowers can be, the purple foliage of Lysimacha ciliata *'Firecracker' makes a dark contrast behind flowers of orange* Crocosmia.

~

parts of the country their shrubby stems are killed off, leaving them to grow from the base or below ground each spring. However, in milder parts, stems may stay alive, giving rise to larger plants.

The Late Summer Border Plan

Some of the plants in the border pictured above left, notably the *Hydrangea* and *Ligularia*, prefer a moist soil and light shade. Those who garden on poor, light soil with borders exposed to the sun should think twice before commiting themselves to these plants. They would need a lot of watering and feeding to look this good. Packing large plants, like the stately *Sorbaria* with its plumes of white flowers, and *Cotinus* with marvellous purple foliage, into a small garden would take courage, but certainly makes a statement. Big plants with bold foliage contribute to a jungle-like, almost tropical atmosphere, even if the plants used are perfectly hardy. The great, leathery, fat, heart-shaped leaves of the *Ligularia* look superb behind the spiky, bright green leaves of *Crocosmia*.

Hydrangeas are great late-summer flowers, if you have the moisture-retentive soil they need. There is also soil pH to take

Planting Guide (see page 42)

1. 3 x *Acaena microphylla,* H: 5 cm (2 in), S: 15 cm (6 in).

2. 3 x *Helenium,* H and S: 90 cm (3 ft).

3. 3 x *Sedum telephium* ssp. *maximum* 'Atropurpureum', H and S: 75 cm (30 in).

4. *Euonymus japonicus* 'Ovatus Aureus', H and S: 1.2 m (4 ft); control by pruning.

5. *Euonymus fortunei* 'Silver Queen', H and S: 1.2 m (4 ft) control by pruning

6. 5 x *Alchemilla mollis* (ladies' mantle), H and S 50 cm (20 in).

7. 3 x Hardy border *Geranium* such as *G. sanguineum,* H and S: 30 cm (12 in).

8. 2 x *Rosa* 'Pink Grootendorst', H and S: 1.5 m (5 ft).

9. *Rosa rugosa* 'Alba', H: 2 m (7 ft), S: 1.5 m (5 ft).

10. *Rosa rugosa* type such as 'Fru Dagmar `Hastrup', H and S: 90 cm (3 ft).

11. *Sorbaria arborea,* H and S: 2.5–4.5 m (8–15 ft).

12. 3 x *Crocosmia* (montbretia), H: 60–90 cm (2–3 ft), S: 25 cm (10 in).

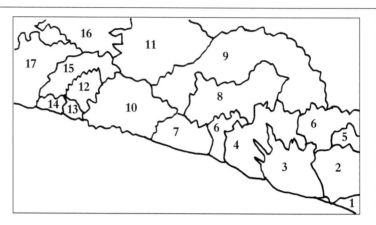

Plot size: length 9 m (30 ft); depth 3 m (10 ft)

13. 3 x *Persicaria affine,* H: 15–30 cm (6–12 in), S: 30 cm (1 ft)

14. 2 x *Hebe albicans,* H: 60 cm (2 ft), S: 90 cm (3 ft)

15. 3 x *Ligularia dentata* 'Desdemona', H and S: 90 cm (3 ft).

16. *Cotinus coggygria* 'Atropurpureus' (smoke bush), H and S: 4.5 m (12 ft).

17. 3 x *Hydrangea macrophylla,* H: 1.5–1.8 m (5–6 ft), S:1.8–2.5 m (6–8 ft) or less with pruning.

into account, for pink-flowered varieties will gradually turn a dingy blue on acid soils, while blues take on a pinkish tinge if the soil is alkaline. There are blueing agents based on aluminium sulphate to bring out the best of blue varieties, while lime can always be added to improve the shades of pinks. However, it makes sense to go with your soil and choose the colours accordingly. For variety, there are lacecaps, which have flatter heads. *H. paniculata,* with a height and spread of 3 m (10 ft), is a marvellous shrub with long-enduring panicles of white flowers which take on a blush of pink as they age. For a splendidly exotic-looking bush, choose *H. villosa* which reaches some 1.8 m (6 ft) or more in height and spread and bears large, soft leaves and wide heads of pale purple flowers opening almost to white on the outside.

Instead of planting ornamental trees and shrubs for late summer, it is worth considering fruit trees like gages, plums, apples and pears. These are both ornamental and productive, giving a display of blossom in spring followed by fruit in late summer and autumn. Full-sized apple trees which might dwarf a small border, causing too much shade, can be eschewed in favour of varieties grafted on to dwarfing rootstocks which reduce the vigour and eventual size of the plant. Given formative pruning in the first few years, dwarf bush-like trees reaching a height and spread of no more than 1.5 m (5 ft) are feasable. Even more useful are minarette trees, which are effectively upright cordons secured to a stake. These can be grown towards the front of a border rather like a living sculpture. Every summer, the season's growth of side shoots are reduced to about 8 cm (3 in) each to keep a pole-like shape, which becomes laden with colourful fruit.

AUTUMN

Autumn is a precious month of glowing light and long shadows, to be cherished before the first severe frost withers the leaves of deciduous plants and kills off the last summer flowers. Where a border is specifically planned for autumn interest, there should be lots of autumn tints, gleaming fruits and fresh, seasonal blooms.

One of the first trees to colour up is *Amelanchier lamarckii,* whose leaves turn bright red. It is a good, small tree, which can eventually reach 6 m (20 ft) in height and spread if grown on a single stem (less

if it is multi-stemmed) and it is covered with masses of star-shaped, white flowers in spring. For gardens with acid soil, *Fothergilla major* is a worthy shrub, with tufts of small, white flowers in spring, and good foliage all summer which turns red, yellow and orange for autumn. It will reach a height of some 1.8–2 m (6–7 ft) and a spread of 1.8 m (6 ft).

Closely related *Hamamelis* (witch hazel), too, can produce amazing colours and will thrive on anything but thin chalky soils. My favourite is *H.* x *intermedia* 'Diane', height and spread 6 m (20 ft), which turns yellow and red in autumn and bears fragrant, spidery, orange-red flowers in winter. It is important to water *Hamamelis* adequately during summer droughts, or its leaves tend to turn brown around the edges and flower buds refuse to form properly for the following winter.

Roses like *R. rugosa,* height and spread 1–2 m (3–6 ft), *R. moyesii* 'Geranium', height 3 m (10 ft) and spread 2.5 m (8 ft), and cultivated forms of *Rosa canina* bear superb hips. *Sorbus* (mountain ash) produce berries of orange, yellow, white or pink, which clash or tone merrily with *Cotoneaster* and *Pyracantha*. For the more unusual, choose *Clerodendrum trichotomum* 'Fargesii', height and spread to 3 m (10 ft), whose sprays of scented summer flowers set into amazing turquoise fruits in bright pink, fleshy calyces. *Euonymus alata* and *E. europaea* (spindle trees), which reach some 1.8–2.5 m (6–8 ft) in height and spread, are equally well-gilded with outrageously flashy, purple fruits with red seeds and red capsules with orange seeds respectively. For bunches of really glowing red berries,

How satisfying to enjoy a final fling of colour from this border, with its lovely scarlet oak and red maple. The colours grade down from the reddish-purple of the rose, through the reds and pinks of Michaelmas daisies and penstemon, to the pale pink of pretty, late-flowering anemones. Variegated foliage and spiky leaves add brightness and texture.

Planting Guide: below
Border Plan: page 48

Planting Guide *(see page 46)*

1. 3 x *Crocosmia* (montbretia),
H: 60–90 cm (2–3 ft), S: 25 cm (10 in).

2. 3 x Deciduous variegated shrub such as
Weigela florida 'Aureovariegata' , H and S: 1.5 m
(5 ft) if stooled annually.

3. Bright pink-red *Penstemon,* such as *P.*
'Garnet', H: 60–75 cm (24–30 in),
S: 60 cm (2 ft).

4. Late-flowering *anemone* such as *Anemone
hupehensis,* H: 75–90 cm (30–36 in),
S: 60 cm (2 ft).

5. 2 x Michaelmas daisy such as *Aster novae-
belgii* 'Patricia Ballard', H: 75–90 cm
(30–36 in), S: 45 cm (18 in).

6. Dark pink Michaelmas daisy, H: 90 cm (3 ft),
S: 45 cm (18 in).

7. *Rosa glauca,* H: 1.8 m (6 ft), S: 1.5 m (5 ft).

8. Michaelmas daisy, H: 1.5 m(6 ft), S: 45 cm
(18 in).

9. Colourful acer such as *Acer rubrum* (scarlet
  maple), H: 6–7.5 m (20–25 ft), S: 2.5–3 m
  (8–10 ft) in 20 years.

10. Background foliage such as *Prunus spinosa*
(blackthorn), H and S: 3–4.5 m (10–15 ft).

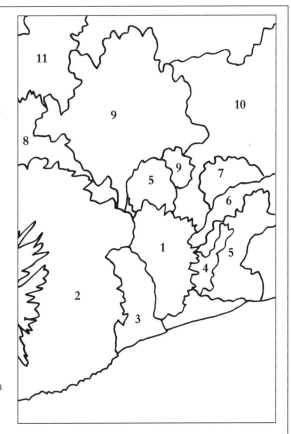

Plot size: length 3 m (10 ft); depth 3 m (10 ft)

11. Oak such as *Quercus coccinea* (scarlet oak), H:
7.5–9 m (25–30 ft), S: 3–4.5 m (10–15 ft) in 20
years, but up to 15 m (50 ft) when fully grown.

plant *Viburnum opulus,* the guelder rose. This will reach 3.5 m (12 ft), but *V. opulus* 'Compactum' grows just 1.5 m (5 ft) tall.

For delightful seed pods try *Staphylea pinnata,* the bladdernut, which, in my opinion, is not planted enough. Tolerant of shade, it succeeds in my garden where I removed an old coal bunker, so it is clearly not fussy about soil. Interesting bark, pretty, white flowers in spring, delicate, pinkish-orange autumn colour plus long-lasting, inflated seed pods are its attributes. Allocate it some space as it reaches a height and spread of some 3.5 m (12 ft). For a fine set of similar pods on a tree, plant *Koelreuteria paniculata,* which reaches 9 m (30 ft) in height and spread in 20 years. It has lovely leaflets and sprays of flowers (hence the name golden rain tree), yellow autumn tints and pink-flushed seed pods.

Glowing colour combinations can be produced by planting pink and mauve Michaelmas daisies. *Aster novi-belgii* varieties, which vary in height from 30 cm (1 ft) to 1.5 m (5 ft), are notorious mildew sufferers and, to be grown well, need early preventative sprayings with an appropriate fungicide. However, this onerous spraying can be sidestepped by growing closely-related asters not prone to this disease. Varieties of *Aster novae-angliae,* the showy New England asters, which usually stand some 75 cm (30 in) tall and spread to 60 cm (2 ft), pass muster, as do shorter *A. amellus,* the Italian starwort. I am very fond of the latter, but it must have a well-drained soil to thrive and is slower to establish itself than some of the others. Choose a variety like mauve-blue 'King

George' or pink 'Sonia'. Another, rather different aster is *A. turbinellus,* which suits a more informal planting and has good drought tolerance. On tall, wiry stems to 1.2 m (4 ft) it opens many small, violet flowers and spreads to 60 cm (2 ft).

The Autumn Border Plan

The plants shown in the picture on page 46 would enjoy a moisture-retentive yet well-drained woodland-type soil, so an annual mulch of leaf mould would work wonders. Full sun or light shade in a position sheltered from wind would be ideal.

Although this planting looks super in autumn, it has the potential to perform well all year round. New growth and spring bulbs will be followed by summer foliage and flowers. After autumn, look forward to a winter of outlines, substituting the *Weigela* with *Cornus alba* 'Spaethii' for red winter stems. This treatment is ideal for a deep corner where two borders meet.

WINTER

There is a surprisingly large number of plants with the ability to delight their owners with flowers, evergreen foliage, colourful stems or interesting bark throughout the winter months. Designing borders for this time of year may be approached in two ways. Plants which are distributed around the garden, entice us outdoors to search them out and sniff their delicate blooms. Or, more spectacularly, borders can be planned for maximum winter impact. Siting this winter garden needs care if the effort is not to be wasted, as plants should be seen from the house or, better still, used to line a well-trod path.

Winter-flowering Plants

Do not be put off by the height of a wall or the depth of a border, as a similar effect can be achieved in smaller spaces. In one front garden I know, a narrow border running along the low boundary wall by the footpath contains a *Mahonia, Cotoneaster horizontalis,* height 90 cm (3 ft) and spread 1.5 m (5 ft), and *Viburnum* x *bodnantense* 'Dawn'. So much prettier than a hedge, they cheer up the whole road in winter. *Viburnums* are superb winter flowerers, opening their pink buds when the weather is mild enough. *V.* x *bodnantense* will grow to a height and spread of 2.75–3.5 m (9–12 ft) but can be kept smaller by periodically pruning away older stems. *V. fragrans* is of similar height and bears paler flowers. Both lose their leaves in winter, which makes their flowers, appearing among bare twigs, even more noticeable.

Other winter-flowering plants include *Abeliophyllum distichum,* which reaches 1.5 m (5 ft) tall and 1.2 m (4 ft) wide trained against the most sheltered fence in my garden. Though the plant is hardy, the beautiful, white, scented flowers which crowd the bare stems are prone to frost damage. Tough and reliable, *Lonicera fragrantissima,* the winter honeysuckle, has a rather ungainly shape, but makes up for this by producing its sweet flowers in the depths of winter. It will reach a height

and spread of 1.8–2.5 m (6–8 ft) if not pruned. For a shady spot near the front door, plant *Sarcococca humilis*, a neat Christmas box, 45 cm (18 in) in diameter. The flowers may be insignificant to the eye, but give off a powerful scent.

Trees for the winter garden should include *Prunus subhirtella* 'Autumnalis', the winter cherry. Though the flowers are small, they open in mild spells throughout winter and are like a breath of spring. Expect it to reach some 5 m (16 ft) in height and spread after ten years, but eventually top 7.5 m (25 ft). An unmissable tree is *Prunus serrula*, the Tibetan cherry. Planted for its rich mahogany-coloured bark, which peels away to reveal ever more brightly coloured, polished layers beneath, it must be sited where winter sun will make it glow. A full-sized tree will reach a height and spread of 9 m (30 ft), but less if grown as a multi-stemmed specimen. Young trees are cut back in the nursery, producing four or five stems.

Many birches have attractive silver, white or pink-toned, peeling bark. Trees can be grown for their young stems, notably varieties of *Salix alba*, like *S. alba* 'Britzensis', whose leaves fall to reveal bright orange stems. Those of *S. alba* 'Vitellina' are bright yellow. Among the dogwoods, *Cornus alba* 'Sibirica' has brilliant red stems and *C. stolonifera* 'Flaviramea' yellow stems. By stooling, or cutting hard back in early spring, all of these can be kept down to a height and spread of some 1.5–1.8 m (5–6 ft). For a less vigorous plant, I have found that on ordinary soils, at least, *C. sanguinea* 'Midwinter Fire' remains a neat 75–90

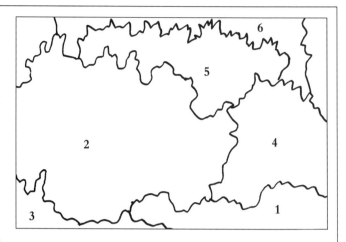

Planting Guide (see page 51)

1. *Hydrangea serrata*, H and S: 1.2 m (4 ft), but can be less if pruned regularly.

2. *Elaeagnus* x *ebbingei* 'Limelight', H and S: 3 m (10 ft).

3. *Osmanthus burkwoodii*, H and S: 1.8–3 m (6–10 ft).

4. *Berberis* x *lologensis* 'Apricot Queen', H and S: 2.5–3 m (8–10 ft).

5. *Mahonia* x *media* 'Winter Sun', H: 3 m (10 ft), S: 1.8 m (6 ft) or less with pruning.

6. *Cotoneaster.*

Plot size: length 3.5 m (12 ft); depth 2.75 m (9 ft)

cm (30–36 in). Although willows are associated with wet soils, my own *S. alba vitellina* 'Britzensis' have tolerated drought conditions in poor soil.

A garden full of dainty winter flowers and colourful stems would still look bare without the density of evergreens and there are many to choose from. Hollies have a great affinity with Christmas and choice of variety is wide, including those with bright, variegated foliage and yellow as well as red berries. For berries to set, a male and female must grow in close proximity. However, *Ilex aquifolium* 'J. C. Van Tol', height 6 m (20 ft) and spread 3.5 m (12 ft), a plain-leaved variety with red berries, will set fruit on its own.

A list of good, reliable, structural evergreens would have to include *Viburnum davidii,* height and spread 1.5 m (5 ft), *Lonicera nitida* 'Baggesen's Gold', height and spread 1.5 m (5 ft), any of the *Elaeagnus, Aucuba japonica* (spotted laurel), height and spread 3 m (10 ft), *Rhamnus alaternus* 'Argenteovariegata', height and spread 3 m (10 ft), and *Osmanthus delavayi,* height and spread 3m (10 ft), with box and yew as hedging.

The real magic of a winter garden comes when the outlines are transformed by a hoar frost. Every leaf, twig and seed head takes on a different character when rimmed with frost and it is worth leaving some of the dead stems on herbaceous perennials in order to enjoy the new lease of life they are given. Some are ugly in winter, but others, like Michaelmas daisies, *Sedum* and *Rodgersia tabularis,* as well as *Buddleia* seed heads, look superb in the right light, offer food for finches and will glisten on frosty mornings.

The Winter Border Plan

Mahonias are the gems of the winter border pictured on page 51. Their

yellow flowers, carried at the ends of stems, are scented as well as cheerful. The leaves are made up of imposing, rather spiny holly-like leaflets of strong, year–round, architectural presence. Pictured in early winter, this border is still benefiting from the last flowers of the hydrangea, its leaves turning red with cold. There is a strong evergreen element with all four major shrubs retaining their leaves through winter. Leaf colour, scented bloom and berries are included in this simple but effective winter composition.

The sunshine colours of Mahonia *flowers and the bright splash of yellow on the leaves of* Elaeagnus *bring this border alight for winter.*

~

Planting Guide: page 50
Border Plan: page 50

Mixed Flower and Vegetable Borders

~

The currently popular idea of mixing fruit, vegetables, flowers and herbs together in borders is successful and worth a try. Not only are many crops attractive, but they also often grow better when surrounded by pretty flowers. This may sound strange, but there are two reasons why this combination is successful. The first is that when crops are interspersed with other plants, especially those with a totally different appearance or smell, it can help deceive potential pests. Imagine a carrot root fly homing in on a crop of carrots or celeriac. Geared for the appearance and smell of that particular crop, the fly is going to be confused if there are brightly coloured flowers or a pungent herb like summer savory growing around or even between the vegetables. I have tried savory in short rows between celeriac plants and it has been a delicious accompaniment to many meals as well as poking through the celeriac foliage (itself attractive), opening tiny purple flowers.

The second reason for success is that flowers, particularly yellow-coloured, flat-topped types like *Limnanthes douglasii* (poached egg plant), height 15 cm (6 in) and spread 10 cm (4 in), and *Calendula* (pot marigold), attract hoverflies and ladybirds. The larvae of these, plus adult ladybirds, are responsible for devouring huge numbers of aphids and can keep them from becoming a serious pest. In the last few decades, vegetable gardening has often been a somewhat sterile process, with long rows of crops separated by barren strips of weeded soil. In smaller gardens and on allotments, many people are changing over to the practice of growing their vegetables in 1.2 m (4 ft) wide beds. Once these have been dug, they need never be trod on again, since it is possible to reach into the middle from either side. An annual mulch of well-rotted compost is all that is needed to keep the soil in good condition.

Whole borders can be treated in this way; you can either plant rows at right angles across a long, narrow border, or divide a deeper one into 1.2 m (4 ft) wide strips. With the vegetables growing closer together, plus interplantings and groups of flowers and herbs, there is also more cover for slug-eating beetles and frogs. However the best way of integrating flowers and vegetables in a border is to use trained fruit trees or soft fruit bushes as structure, then fill in the gaps with small groups of flowers or vegetables at random. Repetition works well, so that instead of having one large patch of French beans, plant two or three round groups, spacing young plants about 10 cm (4 in) apart within each rough circle. As long as the soil is renourished between each planting with well-rotted compost, and fertilizer added for each crop, they will grow well like this.

When sowing straight into the ground,

prepare a patch of empty soil by forking and raking to obtain a fine tilth, then make drills in parallel lines across the patch. Sow the carrots, lettuce, radish, spring onions, rocket or whatever thinly into the rows and gently push the soil back over to cover the seed as described on the seed packet. Thin out and grow on as usual. Suitable crops such as beans, sweetcorn, lettuce, courgettes, tomatoes and curly kale (for winter) can be raised in pots in a cold frame, to be planted out when an area of soil becomes vacant.

In many cases, flowers are used with crops so that they all look good and grow well together, but some of the blooms can also be used for cutting, which is another kind of harvest. Sweet peas, grown around wigwams of canes, are ideal for this, as they need cutting often to make them last. Leaving them on to pod up is a mistake as the supply of new flowers will dwindle. Small bunches of *Calendula,* sweet Williams, *Godetia* and everlastings like *Helichrysum* and *Statice* are great to pick. Herbaceous perennials will yield stems of *Phlox,* lady's mantle, *Bergamot* and *Helenium.*

I find managing small blocks of crops easy. Should groups of peas or broad beans need staking, simply push hazel or other twigs into the ground and bend them towards each other as you would for herbaceous perennials. The young plants will grow up through the twigs, removing the need for stakes and string. For runner beans, push bean poles into the ground in a circle, pulling the tops in and securing them together with wire. Plant a couple of bean seeds (and subse-quently weed one of them out) or a young plant at the foot of each pole and they will quickly climb their support.

Other good management includes remembering not to place the same crop in the same patch of soil the following year, which is rather unlikely. Avoiding this repetitive use of soil helps prevent diseases spreading from one similar crop to the next.

The Mixed Flower and Vegetable Border Plan

Vegetables and fruit require good, well cultivated soil in which to thrive. A sunny position ensures plenty of flowers, good pollination and ripening.

Sweet peas, as shown in the border pictured on page 54, work well as mixed colours, since they all seem to blend well with each other, producing vase after vase of fragrant flowers. *Gypsophila* is invalu-able for adding to larger blooms in vases, especially roses, which rise sumptuously out of a froth of white. Gaps are filled with *Calendula,* which produce a succes-sion of flowers all summer and being hardy annuals, seed themselves around and appear, ready to be thinned out as desired, next spring. There are some lovely shades to choose from, and their progeny are usually reliable. Simply weed out any colours you do not like, to leave only strong, desirable plants, to set seed. A wide range of vegetables sit snugly in amongst the flowers, including the potato 'Kestrel'. This variety is a second early which, planted in early March, will crop

from mid-July onwards and can be stored. I have not tried this myself, but it is a pretty potato with purple eyes, said to have good flavour and resistance to attack by slugs. It is surprising how many potatoes can be harvested from a small area, but they are best suited to growing in rows so that they can be 'earthed up'. This is when soil is dragged up against their stems on each side as the foliage grows, which bolsters them up and helps prevent the tubers near the surface from turning green and inedible.

The practice of growing crops and flowers together will work in the smallest space and can even be employed to fill window boxes.

An A–Z of Crops and Flowers for a Productive Border

Beetroot
What look like single seeds are actually knobbly clusters, but space them 2.5 cm (1 in) apart, thinning later to 8 cm (3 in). Sow bolt-resistant varieties like 'Boltardy' in succession from April until June. Harvest while the roots are young and

Any gardener would feel proud to have an attractive and productive border like this in their garden. The best thing about such borders is that they are changeable and offer the chance to create a different picture of crops and flowers year after year.

~

Planting Guide: page 56
Border Plan: page 53

Planting Guide (see page 54)

1. 10 x Sweet pea 'Galaxy Mixed', H: 2.5 m (8 ft).

2. 10 x *Calendula* 'Touch of Red Mixed', H and S: 38–45 cm (15–18 in).

3. 2 x Courgette 'Zucchini All Green Bush', H: 60 cm (2 ft), S: 90cm (3 ft).

4. Potato 'Kestrel', H and S: 45 cm (18 in); 20 seed potatoes.

5. *Nicandra physaloides* (shoo fly), H: 90 cm (3 ft), S: 30 cm (1 ft).

6. Carrot 'Mokum', H: 20 cm (8 in), S: 8 cm (3 in); 1 packet.

7. Cornflower 'Florence White', H: 35 cm (14 in), S: 23 cm (9 in); 1 packet.

8. Spinach 'Norvak', H: 25 cm (10 in), S: 20 cm (8 in); 1 packet.

9. Celeriac 'Tellus', H and S: 30 cm (1 ft); 1 packet.

10. *Gypsophila* 'Covent Garden White', H and

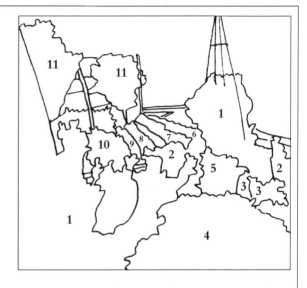

Plot size: length 6 m (20 ft); depth 4.5 m (15 ft)

S: 45 cm (18 in); 1 packet.

11. Apples 'Orleans Reinette' and 'James Grieve', trained as espaliers.

golf-ball sized. Boil the beetroots before skinning them and eat with salads.

Broad Bean

I think broad beans are handsome plants, with their glaucous foliage and attractive flowers, followed by pods. The variety 'Aquadulce Claudia' can be sown in late autumn in milder parts of the country, and will give rise to earlier crops the following year. Spring sowings will yield later crops. Beans can be sown straight into the ground or into containers if the soil is unfit for sowing. Plants usually need support if they are not to flop, and benefit from their soft growing tips being removed once plenty of beans have set.

This often saves them from attack by black fly which love their tender shoots.

French Bean

French beans are great for hot summers, when they will yield many crops of tender beans. I save my space for the narrow 'filet' or 'fine' beans which cost a lot to buy. Wash, top and tail, and these are ready to cook whole, served with a knob of butter. 'Safari' and 'Rido' are both reliable. Plants reach some 23 cm (9 in) tall and look great planted in three groups along the front of a border. Crop them regularly and enjoy their pretty pale flowers. My early summer plants were still cropping in autumn.

Lablab Bean 'Ruby Moon'

This unusual and attractive vegetable, with a long history of cultivation in China, is as easy to grow as late runner beans. Sow seeds in containers during spring and plant them out after the last frosts. Give them the support of a wigwam of canes or bean poles and the lablab beans climb up, producing pretty, pink flowers which turn into glowing maroon pods. They can be cooked just like French or runner beans: pick tender young pods and use them whole or sliced. Older pods become tough and need stringing.

Runner Bean

To provide regular, large platefuls of beans for the table, three to four wigwams of canes are required, but they can be positioned throughout a long border to give it structure. Long hazel poles tied in together at the tops are attractive rustic features, even before the beans have climbed them. Sow in pots during early May, to plant out at the end of the month, or straight into the ground in late May. There are varieties with white, red or pink flowers to choose from and all they need is a rich, well-cultivated soil, plenty of water while the pods are setting, and regular cropping every other day to ensure a long season of production.

Kale

Brassicas (the cabbage family) take up rather a lot of room in borders, though a few pointed, early-spring-sown summer cabbage like 'Hispi' are easy, attractive and quite petite. What I would find space for are six plants of curly kale, planted in two groups of three. Sown in late spring and planted out 60 cm (2 ft) apart in summer, they provide great evergreen foliage and can be cropped over a long period during winter and spring. Try 'Dwarf Green Curled' or 'Tall Green Curled' or, even better, my favourite 'Pentland Brig' which also yields tender shoots in spring.

Kohl Rabi

Kohl rabi are rather like turnips that grow above the soil. Beautiful plants, they make tennis ball-sized globes on the soil's surface, with leaves growing out of them. According to variety, they can be fresh green or purple in colour. Sow small quantities in succession from March to July and either chop up for salads or use in a similar way to turnips. Thin to 8 cm (3 in) apart in their rows.

Leek

Leeks are such a valuable winter crop and are useful for providing interesting winter shape in a mixed ornamental and vegetable border. I usually sow my seeds indoors during late winter or early spring, though a seed bed can be made outdoors when the soil has warmed up in spring. When the young plants are pencil thick, they can be transplanted into their final position, about 15 cm (6 in) apart, during summer. The classic method is to make a deep dibber hole, drop the young plant into this and simply water it to firm it in. This encourages a long, white shaft to form.

Lettuce 'Lollo Mixed'

Out of all the lettuces, I think this mixture is the most attractive and fun to grow. Use the plants to make a decorative edge to a border and crop odd leaves from them rather than taking a whole plant at once. As this type of border is ever-changing, the next sowing could be used to make a weaving strand between two other crops. The seed mixture contains crinkly Italian Lollo types including bright green 'Lollo Verde' and red 'Lollo Rosso'. Growing lettuce is easy, consisting of sowing small quantities of seed into drills every fortnight until midsummer. Thin the seedlings gradually (eating the thinnings as they grow larger) until they are some 20 cm (8 in) apart.

Mixed Annuals

Any hardy annuals are ideal to sow straight into the ground in small patches between crops. However, to make matters simpler, many seed companies have packaged together themed mixtures which can be excellent value. Some are themed according to colour, but there are also cut-flower mixtures, plants likely to attract wildlife and dried flower mixtures.

Parsley

This herb is used in such large quantities during cooking that it is worth growing a lot of it. Like the crinkly lettuce, it makes a superb edging or can be used for ribbon-like patterns in a border. Parsley likes a warm temperature to germinate, so raise the seed under glass, or delay sowing outdoors until the soil has really warmed up in late spring. Some gardeners pour boiling water into the drill to create temperature changes which speed germination Parsley dislikes intensely hot, sunny weather and it is worth growing some in a slightly shady spot in case the summer is very hot.

Peas

Even where there is little space, it is still worth growing small groups of peas. There may not be enough for great platefuls, but there will be sufficient to pick and eat raw, which really is the way to enjoy them. Attractive plants have pretty flowers followed by the pods. Round seeded varieties like 'Feltham First' are hardier and can be sown in early spring. Others are best left until spring is under way and the soil warm. Sow in pots and plant out 10 cm (4 in) apart while very young, or sow straight into the ground. Save twiggy prunings to use as sticks, or buy a bundle of hazel sticks from a garden centre. Try snap and sugar peas too, which can be chopped in their pods and eaten raw in salads.

Rhubarb or Ruby Chard

Ornamental and edible, this chard bears bright red stems which contrast well with its shiny, green foliage. While the leaves have a spinach-like flavour, the stems, which can be cooked separately, have a mild nutty taste. Sow in spring for summer use, or during summer as an attractive autumn crop. The plants become quite large, so thin them gradually so that mature plants are about 30 cm (1 ft) apart. Don't pick whole plants, but continually crop leaves from all the plants so that they remain young and tender.

Ruby or rhubarb chard looks superb teamed with nasturtiums, which of course have edible flowers.

Seakale

A refined crop, seakale also makes an ornamental show with its blue-green leaves and heads of white flowers in early summer. Once plants have established (in two years), they should be covered in early spring, as soon as there are signs of growth, with forcing pots which draw up the pale, young shoots for cropping. Cut them when they are 15–30 cm (6–12 in) high and either eat raw, like celery, or boil lightly until tender and serve like asparagus. Thereafter, remove the forcing pot and allow the plant to grow normally. Strictly speaking, flowers should be removed, but I like them.

Shallot

These are so easy to grow, as small 'seed' shallots are planted 10 cm (4 in) apart in spring with their tips just showing. During the summer, they build up into a clump of plump shallots, which are lifted and dried as soon as growth stops. One of the nicest is pink-fleshed 'Delicato'.

Strawberry

Recently, I have decided to scrap my bed of main-crop strawberries and concentrate on the perpetual or remontant types. These do not produce one bumper crop, but flower and fruit continuously all summer. Instead of gathering bowlfuls over a short period, you can always pick a small handful which can be added to puddings, fruit salads and yoghurt. The best flavour I have come across is from 'Mara des Bois', which has some wild strawberry in its parentage and produces a very flavoursome, aromatic fruit.

Sweetcorn

Corn can be used to add height to a border, as well as yielding sweet, fresh, edible cobs. For really sweet cobs, choose Supersweet varieties and do not mix them with other types. Plant in a circle or block, with the plants just over 30 cm (1 ft) apart, which will ensure a good set within the cobs. They can be sown indoors in early May to be planted out in June, or sown outdoors during late May.

Tomato

The easiest tomatoes to grow outdoors in a border are the bush types, which need neither staking nor their side shoots removed. 'Red Alert' is a good, small-fruited variety and a couple of plants will produce plenty of tasty fruit for salads. For a small quantity, it is best to buy small plants, planting them out at the beginning of June. Give them a feed of tomato fertilizer every week once their fruits are setting.

Colour-themed Borders

~

Using colour themes for borders has become widely popular, inspired by larger-scale plantings in famous gardens. Most notable is the white border at Sissinghurst Castle in Kent and perhaps the amazing red borders at Hidcote Manor in Gloucestershire. Gardeners are continuously creating works of art by placing plants together, but we have to be a patient breed. No sooner does one magical composition reach its crescendo than time destroys it until another year. In larger gardens, there is space for whole borders to peak at once, but there needs to be more caution in smaller spaces. Here a succession of small triumphs and cleverly planned seasonal changes are important if year-round interest is to be maintained.

Planting according to colour is a good discipline, enabling all sorts of combinations to be tried out. In small borders, this need not be too strictly applied: choose perhaps two or three colours which blend well together. Sometimes plants dictate this by changing colour according to season. The lovely, yellow-leaved *Rubus cockburnianus* 'Golden Vale', for instance, will shed its leaves in autumn to reveal ghostly, silver stems 1.2–1.5 m (4–5 ft) in height and spread. Purple fennel, planted for its mass of feathery leaves in summer, eventually rises up to heads of tiny, yellow flowers. Purple and yellow combine well, so take

advice from nature and consider using their contrasting shades as a theme. If you are planting a mixed border of trees, shrubs, perennials and annuals, it is a good idea to pick a colour from the main trees and shrubs, then repeat it throughout the smaller plantings. Take into account not only leaf and flower colour, but also autumn tints and winter stems.

Although gardeners are free to create their own artistic rules in colour-coded borders, there is one useful discipline. Within all colours there are warm and cold tones. Take a look at yellow, for instance. Some yellows are warm and buttery. Others have that tinge of green which gives them a cold, acid appearance. When combining colours, I find that, generally, placing warm tones together, or cold tones together, works better than mixing them all up.

The golden-leaved form of the flowering currant, *Ribes sanguineum* 'Brocklebankii', sprouts a fine crop of acid-yellow leaves in spring, closely followed by pink flowers. A small shrub, it reaches a height and spread of about 90 cm (3 ft). In front, I have planted a mass of feathery-leaved *Dicentra* 'Stuart Boothman', height 45 cm (18 in) and spread 30 cm (1 ft), whose show of pink flowers lasts from spring right into late summer. When many of the *Euphorbia* (spurges) flower, their whole inflorescence

Silver, pink and purple are colours which com-
bine together particularly well. It is the mix of
definite shapes, ground cover and dainty,
informal flowers that make this
border so pretty.

∽

Planting Guide: page 63
Border Plan: page 64

turns a bright acid-yellow which contrasts dramatically with other electric
colours like the bright, cold pinks and
purples produced by some of the hardy
geraniums. Best of all is *Geranium* 'Ann
Folkard', height 50 cm (20 in) and spread
90 cm (3 ft), whose almost climbing
stems produce leaves glowing with acid-
yellow when young and are dotted with
brilliant, dark-centred, magenta flowers

Planting Guide (see page 62)

1. 6 x *Geranium traversii* var. *elegans* (hardy border geranium), H: 20 cm (8 in), S: 30 cm (1 ft).

2. 2 x *Artemisia pontica* (Roman wormwood), H: 60 cm (2 ft), S: 20 cm (8 in).

3. *Artemisia arborescens*, H: 90 cm (3 ft), S: 75 cm (30 in).

4. 3 x *Lychnis coronaria* 'Alba' (madam pinch-me-quick), H: 60 cm (2 ft), S: 45 cm (18 in).

5. 7 (each side) x *Stachys byzantina* 'Big Ears' syn. *S. lanata* (lamb's ears), H: 38 cm (15 in), S: 60 cm (2 ft).

6. 2 x *Berberis thunbergii* 'Atropurpurea Nana', H and S: 60 cm (2 ft).

7. 2 x *Astrantia maxima* (masterwort), H: 60 cm (2 ft), S: 45 cm (18 in).

8. *Santolina chamaecyparissus* (cotton lavender), H: 75 cm (30 in), S: 90 cm (3 ft).

9. 3 x *Anemone hupehensis japonica*, H: 75 cm (30 in), S: 45 cm (18 in).

10. *Artemisia canescens*, H: 45 cm (18 in,) S: 30 cm (1 ft).

11. *Dianthus* (pink) such as 'Doris', H: 15 cm (6 in), S: 30 cm (1 ft).

12. 3 x *Elymus hispidus* syn. *E. glaucus* (blue lyme grass), H: 60 cm (2 ft), S: extensive.

13. *Iris ensata* 'Rose Queen', H and S: 60–90 cm (2–3 ft).

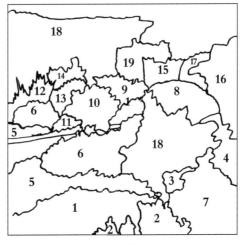

Plot size (each strip): length 2.75 m (9 ft); depth 1.8 m (6 ft)

14. *Rosa* 'Nathalie Nypels', H and S: 90 cm (3 ft).

15. *Achillea millefolium* 'Lilac Beauty' (yarrow), H and S: 60 cm (2 ft).

16. *Rosa* 'Comte de Chambord', H and S: 1.2 m (4 ft).

17. *Pittosporum tenuifolium* 'Tom Thumb', H and S: 75 cm (30 in).

18. *Prunus cerasifera* 'Nigra' grown as a hedge, 2 m (7 ft) high.

19. 3 x *Phlox paniculata*, H: 3 ft (90 cm)S: 2 ½ ft (75 cm)

produced right through the summer.

I'm not generally keen on *Carex comans* 'Bronze', which grows to 45 cm (18 in) tall with a spread of 38 cm (15 in), a rather stiff-looking, brown-leaved grass which some gardeners adore. To me, it can look as if it is permanently dying off, but I allow it in the garden because it forms half of a very satisfying partnership. The pinkish-brown leaves can seem almost welcoming as a mellow backdrop to dusky pink *Echinacea purpurea* 'Magnus' (purple cone flower), which achieves a height of 60–90 cm (2–3 ft) and a spread of 45 cm (18 in), and the two strike up a lively composition in late summer.

SILVER, PINK AND PURPLE

Plantings of pink, purple and silver create a shimmering haze which I find most satisfying in the heat of midsummer. My garden being on a thin, dry soil which suits many silvery-leaved drought-tolerant plants, I seem to find this colour combination happening almost by chance, again and again. Even on more moisture-retentive soils, it is not difficult to find suitable plants for the same effect.

My favourite combination takes place on a slightly mounded border, the end of which juts out into the lawn like a peninsula. Here *Rosa glauca* (syn. *rubrifolia*) provides height and sets the style with its red stems and grey, purple-tinged leaves. Single, pink flowers are white-centred and give way to a display of red hips. This will eventually reach a height and spread of some 1.8 m (6 ft) and will form an important contour in a border which, further round, contains *Cercis siliquastrum* (Judas tree), height 4.5–6 m (15–20 ft) and spread 9 m (30 ft), and cooking apple 'Annie Elizabeth', height 4.5 m (15 ft) and spread 5.5 m (18 ft). Around the rose are planted *Teucrium fruticans* (germander), height 1.2–1.5 m (4–5 ft) and spread 1.2 m (4 ft), which covers the ground with its silvery stems and leaves, *Eryngium bourgatii* (sea holly), height 45–60 cm (18–24 in) and spread 30 cm (1 ft), and *Picea pungens* 'Glauca Procumbens', height 45 cm (18 in) and spread 1.8 m (6 ft), a slow-growing prostrate spruce. Then among these are sprinkled *Lavandula stoechas* 'Marshwood', height and spread 75 cm (2½ ft), *Foeniculum vulgare* 'Purpureum' (purple fennel), height 1.5 m (5 ft) and spread 45 cm (18 in), and a lovely selection of seed-raised thrifts known as *Armeria formosa*, large-flowering hybrids which flower faithfully year after year. There are also mats of long-flowering *Silene schafta,* with a height of 10–15 cm (4–6 in) and spread of 15 cm (6 in).

The Silver, Pink and Purple Border Plan

This border is illustrated on page 62. Most people wanting a purple hedge choose *Fagus sylvatica* 'Riversii' (purple beech). It is a superb hedging plant, with glowing purple leaves becoming even richer in autumn. This border is backed by a more unusual but no less worthy hedge of *Prunus cerasifera* 'Nigra', the reddish-purple cherry plum or myrobalan. Though not so handsome during autumn and winter, it has the compensation of pale pink blossom in early spring. With either choice, be prepared to wait some five to six years for a hedge to form.

This border will peak in June, but will be of strong structural interest from summer through to December. It is then that the berberis will have lost all of its leaves and, although evergreen, the *Stachys, Santolina* and *Artemisia* begin to look sad and wintry. From midwinter onwards strong design shapes pay dividends, for although there is nothing planted specifically for winter interest, the outlines of hedge, shingle path and edging work well during the quiet season. A sharp hoar frost can transform the shapes of dormant plants into a fairy-tale scene for a day or two.

Dwarf *Berberis* are naturally dumpling-shaped and will need no training to achieve this. Cotton lavender needs more help and will require a severe pruning back in spring to create a dense head of aromatic, silvery foliage. *Artemisias,* too, need cutting back in spring if they have become straggly. They are short-lived plants, so plan to replace them after three or four years. *Stachys byzantina* regenerates itself easily, producing new growth in spring, and will need only a little tidying to keep it under control. It rises up into sprays of small, pink flowers towards the end of summer, which is pretty but would destroy the carpet-like quality of the felty leaves. Removing developing flower stems will discourage such wayward behaviour.

Dark and light pink roses add quality and perfume to the scene, while the dainty flowers of *Astrantia* and *Lychnis* thread their way through other plants. Be sure to select the soft, white form of *Lychnis coronaria*, or you will end up with a bright pink shocker. Plantings of *Achillea* and Japanese anemone will ensure that pink flowers will carry on right into late summer and early autumn.

COOL GREEN

Borders based simply on shades of green can be effective and soothing. I know whole gardens which rely on this year-round greenery, lightened here and there by pockets of seasonal annuals and bulbs.

The Cool Green Border Plan

The plants shown in the photograph on page 66 are not fussy about soil type and will perform well in sun or light shade. *Bergenia, Alchemilla mollis* and *Prunus laurocerasus* will tolerate deeper shade.

Robinia pseudoacacia 'Frisia' is a small tree which has become deservedly popular for its bright green leaflets. A clever gardener I know has weighted the branches of a young tree down with large stones used as cogs. As they grow, he winds the strings around the cogs to bring them down a little tighter. The result has been to create a weeping tree ideal for a small space.

Here the robinia forms a focal point for a small path used to cut the border in two. A clever tactic for a deep border, it opens up possibilities of more interesting planting both within the borders and as an edging along the paths. Two bold shrubs of evergreen *Elaeagnus* x *ebbingei* 'Gilt Edge' will ensure winter interest, but the plants have been treated differently. One has been allowed to merge naturally with the background, while that towards the front has been shaped by clipping out taller stems. It is important to check variegated forms of *Elaeagnus* regularly to make sure that no shoots have reverted to plain green. These should be cut back to their point of origin or the whole plant will gradually revert to green.

Managing the height of the *Elaeagnus* has created a clear view to the *Pyracantha* (firethorn) beyond. Another evergreen, its masses of white flowers give way to, in this case, yellow berries which last well through the winter. Autumn is also

Planting Guide *(see above)*

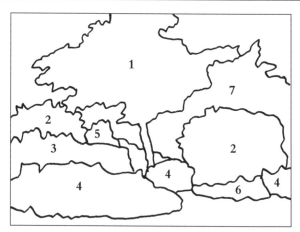

1. *Robinia pseudoacacia* 'Frisia', H: 6 m (20 ft), S: 3 m (10 ft) in 20 years.

2. *Elaeagnus* x *ebbingei* 'Gilt Edge', H and S: 3 m (10 ft).

3. *Prunus laurocerasus* 'Zabeliana', H: 1.2 m (4 ft), S: 2.5 m (8 ft).

4. 20 x *Alchemilla mollis* (lady's mantle), H and S: 50 cm (20 in).

5. *Rhus typhina* 'Dissecta' (sumach), H and S: 3.5 m (12 ft).

6. 3 x *Bergenia* 'Silberlicht' (elephant's ears), H: 45 cm (18 in), S: 60 cm (2 ft).

7. *Pyracantha atalantioides* 'Aurea' (firethorn), H: 5 m (16 ft), S: 3.5 m (12 ft).

Plot size: length 5.5 m (18 ft); depth 2.75 m (9 ft)

catered for by *Rhus typhina* 'Dissecta' (sumach) which will transform the border with its fiery red-orange tints.

Alchemilla mollis (lady's mantle) makes a wonderful edging plant for paths, whose edges become masked by a foam of yellow flowers which persist all summer, gradually fading to brown. The plant dies down for winter, but bounces back in spring, when the perfection of its leaves, whose points are beaded with glistening drops of water in the morning, is most noticeable. Spring is the best time to dig up old plants, and divide and replant them to cover larger areas. Over a few years, one alchemilla can go a long way. For a neat, evergreen border, *Bergenia* (elephant's ears) is superb. Many varieties turn rich red in winter and stems of white, pink or red flowers are sent up in spring. All of these plants are well able to tolerate the dappled shade created by trees around the border. This is a large, deep border but the planting ideas could work in smaller spaces if numbers are reduced.

Green flowers

There are quite a few green-flowered plants which could be used to create a subtle, green-shaded planting in a small border.

White, double tulips make an ideal partner for the evergreen foliage of variegated Euonymus *and the tiered branches of* Viburnum plicatum f. tomentosum, *bearing flat heads of white flowers.*

For spring, *Daphne laureola* (spurge laurel) takes some beating. A slow-growing evergreen, it will eventually reach 90 cm (3 ft) high and slightly more across. In February, bunches of pale green flowers open. They are scented, but you have to get close in order to detect their sweet fragrance, which tends to be more marked during the evening. In my garden it has proved to be tolerant of both shade and competition from roots in a rather dry spot.

Ribes laurifolium, height and spread 1.5 m (5 ft), is another evergreen, but with a more lax habit. Pendent racemes of pale yellowish-green flowers are produced in late winter, which contrast well with the foliage. Hellebores, too, are effective, but need to be planted *en masse* for a real show. *H. lividus* subsp. *corsicus* bears pale green flowers on plants 60 cm (2 ft) tall and with slightly less spread. Deep and lime green are tempting colours to match with yellow and bronze. In spring, *Epimedium* x *versicolor* 'Sulphureum', height and spread 30 cm (1 ft), makes a superb patch of spectacularly bronzed new foliage joined by sprays of pendent yellow flowers. It is best to shear off the old foliage, which reaches about 30 cm (1 ft) at the end of winter, to make way for this superb new growth. Again, several plants are needed to create impact.

For summer, clumps of green flowers in a border can be provided by sowing seeds of *Nicotiana* (tobacco plants) in spring. Those to choose are *Nicotiana* 'Lime Green', which bears acid green flowers which spread to 30 cm (1 ft) atop stems some 60 cm (2 ft) tall. For more height, go for *N. langsdorffii* which bears

elegant sprays of smaller, nodding flowers spreading to 30 cm (1 ft) on plants 1–1.5 m (3–5 ft) tall. Plant out at the end of May when there is little danger of frost, and they will flower all summer.

RED AND YELLOW

Borders based on warm, fiery shades of red, orange and yellow are easy and great fun to create. There are so many good, strong herbaceous perennials and annuals in this category that the gardener is almost spoilt for choice. It is especially satisfying if the border can be designed to peak at the end of summer, when so many gardens which triumphed in June are looking second rate.

For those wishing to create a mixed border, including warm-toned shrubs, deciduous *Cotinus coggygria* 'Notcutt's Variety' is a smoke bush reaching a height and spread of 3.5 m (12 ft) with bright-reddish purple leaves. It will lose its leaves in winter. Evergeen *Nandina domestica*, the sacred bamboo, becomes tinged with red in winter and some of these leaves persist to give it a touch of warmth during summer. Site away from wind and the plants will grow to a height and spread of 1.8 m (6 ft). On a smaller scale, *Potentilla* 'Red Ace' bears bright red flowers at only 90 cm (3 ft) tall and with a similar spread.

Sunflowers of all shapes and colours, from yellow to russet and red, are excellent gap fillers and there is a superb plant for the back of a border that is not grown enough. I first saw *Tithonia rotundifolia* growing in Monet's garden at Giverny.

Easy to grow from spring-sown seed, the variety 'Torch' reaches a good 1.2 m (4 ft), is self-supporting and bears silky stems of bright orange flowers 8 cm (3 in) in diameter.

The Red and Yellow Border Plan

The plants shown in the photograph on page 70 would appreciate a rich but well-drained soil and plenty of sunshine during the summer and autumn.

At the back of this border is a distinctive shrub rose, whose flask-shaped hips are yellow and orange. *Rosa moyesii* 'Geranium' bears single, scarlet blooms in summer, followed by these elegant

hips on a bush that slowly reaches a height of 3 m (10 ft).

No hot border would be complete without its backing of stately *Kniphofia* (red hot pokers). The classic variety *K.* 'Royal Standard' is tall, but there are many varieties available in a range of heights. Also indispensible is trendy *Dahlia* 'Bishop of Llandaff', whose red flowers are an ideal accompaniment to deep purple foliage, making a dramatic dark mass in the border. I leave my dahlia tubers in the soil for winter, and so far they have come up year after year. If I gardened on a heavier soil, in a colder district, I would almost certainly lift them, store them frost-free and plant them out in April. I may come unstuck one year, but this method does save time

Planting Guide (see page 70)

1. 3 x *Rudbeckia fulgida* var. *deanii* H: 90 cm (3 ft), S: 60 cm (2 ft).

2. 3 x Rhubarab chard H: 60 cm (2 ft), S: 45 cm (18 in).

3. 3 x *Monarda didyma* such as 'Mrs. Perry' (bergamot), H: 90 cm (3 ft), S: 45 cm (18 in).

4. 3 x *Verbena* 'Lawrence Johnston', H and S: 23 cm (9 in).

5. 5 x *Nicotiana* such as 'Nicki Bright Pink' (tobacco plant), H and S: 30 cm (1 ft).

6. 3 x *Dahlia* 'Bishop of Llandaff', H and S: 90 cm (3 ft).

7. Red *Dahlia*, such as 'Grenadier', H: 1.2 m (3–4 ft), S: 90 cm (3 ft).

8. 2 x *Kniphofia* 'Samuel's Sensation' (red hot poker), H: 1.2 m (4 ft), S: 90 cm (3 ft).

9. *Crocosmia masoniorum* (montbretia),

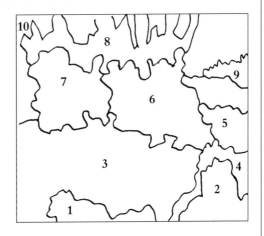

Plot size: length 3.5 m (12 ft); depth 2.75 m (9 ft)

H: 1.5 m (5 ft), S: 45 cm (18 in).

10. *Rosa moyesii* 'Geranium', H: 3 m (10 ft), S: 2.5 m (8 ft)

Follow this recipe using an exciting mixture of red, yellow and orange to create a sizzling hot red border.

∼

Planting Guide: page 69
Border Plan: page 69

and is one less job to think about. Among dahlias, generally, there are plenty of warm colours available in a variety of shapes and sizes. Small- to medium-sized flower heads suit herbaceous borders better than the enormous kinds, which I feel are best grown to one side in a show of their own.

Masses of flat-headed *Achillea,* tall late-flowering yellow *Heliopsis,* spiky-leaved *Crocosmia* (montbretia) and brilliant red *Monarda* (bergamot) are reliable herbaceous perennials. It is amazing how quickly a few small plants spread into large clumps. Be prepared to tackle *Heliopsis* regularly, as it tends to send roots everywhere, putting up stems where least expected.

This is a deep border, which makes the

planting even more effective. However, the arrangement could easily be scaled down by planting just one of each plant and keeping the clumps smaller by regular division and replanting.

There are so many good plants to grow as annuals that it is worth saving some gaps for them. Keeping pockets for these brings the opportunity to ring the changes. It is all very well to create whole borders of one or two colours for the summer, but more circumspect planting is needed for smaller gardens, where space is at a premium. Too many flowering herbaceous perennials and annuals means little to enjoy during the winter months, so greater emphasis is placed on shrubs to give structure.

PURPLE

It is hard to believe that there are so many shades of one colour until you plant up a themed border with different flowers. Within the

Shades of purple, mauve and blue lightened by lime green and a splash of yellow from the pansies, create a cool border. The stems and leaves of alliums and silvery foliage of artemisia add touches of silver-grey to the picture.

~

Planting Guide: page 72
Border Plan: above

range of purple, mauve and lilac there are enough subtle changes to make a border come alive. Plantings like this contain so much refinement of light and dark shades that even on dull days it always appears as though the sun is catching the petals.

The Purple Border Plan

Good, well-drained soil and a sunny position will suit the plants pictured directly below.

Planting Guide (see page 71)

1. 36 x Pansies, H and S: 20 cm (8 in) and 25 x *Myosotis* (forget-me-not), H and S: 20 cm (8 in).

2. 3 x *Allium karataviense*, H: 20–25 cm (8–10 in), S: 25–30 cm (10–12 in).

3. *Rosa* 'Mary Rose' (pink-flowered modern shrub), H and S: 1.2 m (4 ft).

4. *Rosa* 'Fritz Nobis' (pink-flowered modern shrub), H: 1.5 m (5 ft), S: 1.2 m (4 ft).

5. *Euphorbia lathyrus* (caper spurge), H: 60–120 cm (2–4 ft), S: 30–60 cm (1–2 ft).

6. 3 x *Polemonium caeruleum* (Jacob's ladder), H: 75 cm (30 in), S: 60 cm (2 ft).

7. *Geranium sylvaticum*, H: 90 cm (3 ft), S: 60 cm (2 ft).

8. 3 x *Artemisia ludoviciana* 'Valerie Finnis', H: 90 cm (3 ft), S: 60 cm (2 ft).

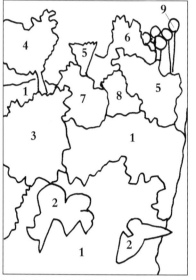

Plot size: length 3.5 m (12 ft); depth 1.8 m (6 ft)

9. 7 x *Allium hollandicum* 'Purple Sensation', H: 75 cm (30 in), S: 20 cm (8 in).

Late spring is a lovely time in the garden before the summer droughts, when plants seem young and fresh. This riot of pansies and *Myosotis* (forget-me-not) would have been planted the previous autumn from seed sown in the summer. The effect of the mingled flowers is jewel-like. Among these, *Allium* throw up their flower spikes like firework displays from bulbs also planted last autumn. It is important to cover the bulbs by three times their own depth with soil. *Allium karataviense* sends up a short flower stalk crowned by a rounded head some 15 cm (6 in) across of pale lilac flowers, which show up beautifully against the wide, glaucous leaves. At only 20–25 cm (8–10 in) high, they are well suited to the front of a border. For stature, choose *A. hollandicum*, or *A. hollandicum* 'Purple Sensation', whose 10 cm (4 in) wide heads of purple flowers are held 75 cm (30 in) high. Good choices would also include *A. giganteum*, which can get up to 1.8 m (6 ft) tall and *A. christophii*, whose football-like heads of flowers are 20 cm (8 in) across and reach 60 cm (2 ft) high.

Others stars of this border include *Polemonium caeruleum* (Jacob's ladder), a herbaceous perennial which flowers year after year, and the hardy geranium. Later flower colour will be provided by roses.

One curious plant, again with that lime green that seems to go so well with the purple colour range, is *Euphorbia lathyrus* (caper spurge). This seeds itself around in gardens, often coming up where it has never been seen before. An attractive curiosity, it is said to deter moles. Do not be fooled by its common name into eating its seed pods, as it is poisonous. Sometimes, rather too many caper spurge seedlings will set in one border, in which case thin them out while they are still young.

In a smaller, narrower border, this colourful mass of pansies and *Myosotis* can be effectively interspersed with some of the shorter *Alliums*. You will find all these set seedlings on their own and with careful management will be self-perpetuating.

Using Colour

The great thing about colour-themed borders is that a complete redesign and replant is not always necessary. Good borders usually have a strong backbone of shrubs and these can take the lead. If, for instance, *Viburnum plicatum* f. *tomentosum*, height 3 m (10 ft) and spread 3.5 m (12 ft), is already established, its horizontal branches will come alive with heads of white flowers in late spring. Build on this by planting around it with *Euonymus fortunei* 'Silver Queen', height 2.4 m (8 ft) and spread 1.5 m (5 ft), which enjoys a slightly climbing habit and will send its stems up into the *Viburnum* (see picture on page 67). Add to this a beautiful, double-flowered, white tulip and for a month a visual feast of fresh green and white can be enjoyed. Carry this idea on around the garden and, even in a small space, a succession of similar tableaux can be delivered throughout the year.

In my garden, an *Elaeagnus pungens* 'Maculata', height and spread 3.6 m (12ft), provides inspiration for one section of border. Its gold-variegated, evergreen leaves are good all year, but particularly welcome in winter. During summer, the yellow in the leaf is picked up by the flower heads of *Phlomis russeliana*, height 90 cm (3 ft) and spread 60 cm (2 ft), which makes worthy ground cover. Further on, *Juniperus* x *media* 'Pfitzeriana Aurea', height 90 cm (3 ft) and spread 1.8 m (6 ft), is, again, tinged with yellow and makes a year-round, prostrate shape.

Elsewhere, the dominant plant is a small tree, *Cercis canadensis* 'Forest Pansy', the eastern redbud. It is supposed to reach a height and spread of 9 m (30 ft), but in my garden the branches seem weak and whole sections have pulled away from the main trunk and died. Nevertheless, it remains a large shrub and is not a bad shape. In spring, pink buds appear all over the stems, opening to pink, pea-like flowers. As they open, reddish-purple, heart-shaped leaves begin to unfold all over the tree. In front of this, *Cynara cardunculus* (cardoon) makes a silvery mound, sending its stems of large, thistle-like flowers to 1.8 m (6 ft) in height and 90 cm (3 ft) in spread. Then a mass of the wonderful biennial *Salvia sclarea* 'Turkestanica' picks up all these colours. Mauve and white flowers surrounded by pink bracts make a haze above sage-green leaves, the plants reaching a height of 90 cm (3 ft) and a spread of about 30 cm (1 ft), before their finale with seed pods which rattle crisply in the breeze.

Borders for Wildlife

~

To me, the wildlife in my garden is as much an attraction as the trees, shrubs, flowers, fruit and vegetables I grow. Fond though I am of my plants, the added pleasures of watching beetles scurrying, spiders building their webs, bees visiting flowers and birds foraging for food cannot be overestimated. It is possible to encourage plenty of wildlife into a garden without turning it into a wilderness. All that is required is a basic understanding of how the ecological system that is your garden actually works.

In some ways, gardens cannot be called natural, because we gather together plants from all over the world in a tiny space that is often distanced from natural countryside by many other gardens. But then a great percentage of our natural countryside has been fiddled about with by man anyway. Gardens often stand a greater chance of supporting a wide range of life than open fields of crops fed with artificial fertilizers and sprayed with pesticides.

Although worms, which leave their

A mass of nectar-rich flowers is sure to attract local butterflies. They appreciate sunny, sheltered borders.

~

Planting Guide: page 76
Border Plan: page 76

Planting Guide (see page 74)

1. *Buddleia davidii* (butterfly bush), H and S: 4.5 m (15 ft), less with pruning.

2. 5 x *Aster* such as 'Prinette Pink', H and S: 60 cm (2 ft).

3. 3 x *Veronica spicata* (spiked speedwell), H: 60 cm (2 ft), S: 45 cm (18 in).

4. 3 x *Verbena* 'Silver Anne', H: 15–20 cm (6–8 in), S: 45 cm (18 in).

5. *Aster frikartii* 'Monch' (Michaelmas daisy),H: 75 cm (30 in), S: 45 cm (18 in).

6. 5 x *Dahlia*, H and S: 1.2–1.5 m (4–5 ft).

7. 3 x *Dahlia*, H: 60 cm (2 ft), S: 45 cm (18 in).

8. *Rosa* 'Magenta' (modern shrub rose), H: 1.5 m (5 ft), S: 1.2 m (4 ft).

9. *Rosa* such as Jacqueline du pré (modern

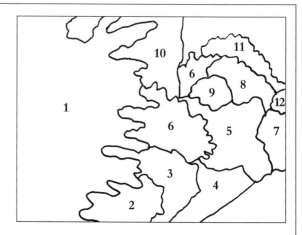

Plot size: length 6 m (20 ft); depth 2.5 m (8 ft)

shrub) H and S: 1.5 m (5 ft).

10. *Clematis viticella* 'Etoile Violette', H: 3 m (10 ft).

11. *Salvia sclarea* 'Turkestanica' H: 1.2 m (4 ft), S: 90 cm (3 ft).

casts all over the lawn, slugs which ravage our hostas and aphids which infest young shoots are a nuisance, they also provide food for birds. When a large population of birds gets into the habit of treating your garden like a larder, you will have fewer pests and the time-consuming and costly need to control them will largely disappear. Succeeding with this philosphy depends on being able to distinguish the goodies from the baddies. Shiny, black ground beetles which attack and eat slugs are to be encouraged. Spiders clear up a lot of flies and other garden pests and a rich population of them is beneficial too.

If gardeners who habitually reach for chemical controls whenever there is a problem just take a step back for a couple of seasons, they might be amazed at the results. Avoid being over-tidy in the garden too, as pieces of wood, stones and the dry stems of dead herbaceous perennials create the hiding places which many creepy-crawlies rely on for their cover.

The Wildlife Border Plan

A well-conditioned neutral soil will suit the plants pictured on page 74. Site flowers in full sun to attract butterflies and facilitate a good set of seeds for the birds.

This late summer border is teeming with flowers in all shades of pink and purple. Not only are these good garden plants, but many are also the favourites of butterflies, especially peacock, red admiral, comma, small tortoiseshell and some of the fritillaries which visit the garden, their wings a vibrant orange-brown. Buddleia and a column groaning with purple clematis are the main features, with roses planted between and the gaps filled with *Dahlia, Veronica* and *Salvia sclarea* 'Turkestanica'. This distinctive plant is grown as a biennial. Aromatic leaves and flowers rise up in a shimmering mass during midsummer, leaving behind a crop of dry, rustling seed pods. Leave them to shed seed and many seedlings will spring up around old plants. *Sedum* and Michaelmas daisies are more butterfly favourites. Leave the seed heads on buddleia and they will be a source of food for birds.

Even narrow borders can be planted to attract wildlife. Concentrate on nectar-rich plants, grown in smaller clumps. Continuous soil cover will create a haven for frogs, toads and ground beetles.

Butterfly Borders

Enjoying a large population of butterflies in your garden depends on two points. First, and most importantly, there must be a wild area nearby where butterflies can breed and use as cover. Many popular types like small tortoiseshell, red admiral, comma and peacock lay their eggs on nettles, which the caterpillars subsequently eat. Painted ladies prefer thistles, while the gatekeeper and meadow brown feed on grasses. The holly blue lays its first lot of eggs on holly and the second brood feeds on ivy. One of the first butterflies to appear in spring is the yellow

brimstone. This lovely butterfly overwinters as an adult, hiding within deep clumps of brambles. It lays its eggs on buckthorn or alder. Orange tips overwinter as cocoons attached to grass stems and the butterflies lay their eggs on lady's smock and garlic mustard.

If there are no local wild areas, it may be possible to plant some of these food plants in the garden and leave areas of natural grass for butterflies to use. A point worth mentioning is that butterflies like shelter, so food plants for caterpillars plus nectar plants for adults need to be out of wind and in the sun. Tucking a group of nettles around the dark, cold side of a house will not attract butterflies, because they are looking for warmth and sunshine.

The second important point when setting out to attract butterlies is, of course, the nectar source of flowers which attract the adults themselves. If there is a good population of butterflies in the area, simply providing a good larder of their favourite flowers in the garden will ensure that you see masses of colourful fluttering wings all summer. Again, make sure their favourites are positioned in the sun.

The best-known butterfly flower must be *Buddleia davidii,* with a height and spread of 5 m (15 ft), often known as the butterfly bush. There is a good range of colours available, from white, through pale lilac, to deep purple and reddish-purple. Use them as backbone plants for a sunny border. *Buddleia davidii* is accommodating when it comes to pruning. If they are flopping around in autumn, they can be pruned hard then to tidy them up. An early spring pruning is more conventional,

This attractive pond will ensure an even greater population of frogs, toads, newts, drag-onflies and other insects. Birds can use the water for bathing and drinking. Note the dense ground cover of the planting, which creates ideal shade for amphibians.

but if they are pruned again in late spring, it will delay flowering to guarantee that there are plenty of blooms around when the late hatchings of butterflies are on the wing. Pretty much all the buddleias attract butterflies, including graceful lilac-purple-flowered *B. alternifolia*, height 6 m (20 ft), which has narrow, grey-green leaves and a pendent habit. Orange-yellow flowered *B.* x *weyerana* is delightful, reaching a height and spread of up to 3.5 m (12 ft).

Late-flowering *Ceanothus* 'Gloire de Versailles', height and spread 1.5 m (5 ft), one of the Californian lilacs, is also well visited. Other favourites include *Helenium,* teasel, *Scabious*, sweet rocket,

wallflowers, *Sedum spectabile* and *Liatris*. The most important thing is to have nectar flowers opening from spring right through to autumn.

Borders for Birds

There is a common misconception that you must put food out to attract birds. This certainly helps in winter, but if you embrace the idea of reducing the use of garden chemicals to an absolute min-imum, there will be plenty of insect life around for them to feed on for most of the year. For other birds, the right mix-ture of plants will ensure a good supply of seeds and fruits. In most gardens, blackbirds and song thrushes can be seen picking worms and other grubs out of lawns. These birds have become scarcer in some gardens recently, but nobody is quite sure why. Fingers have been pointed at an increase in the magpie population (they will prey on the eggs and young of other birds), but not conclusively. Flocks of starlings also feed from lawns and, with blackbirds, enjoy feasting on fallen apples, which also attract late butterflies.

Goldfinches perform acrobatics on seed heads, greenfinches tuck into rowanberries and in winter, when apple trees are bare of leaves, you can easily see the antics of blue, great and long-tailed tits as they forage for overwintering aphids. If you live near wooded areas you may also be rewarded by visits from woodpeckers, nuthatches and tree creepers which are a joy to see in gardens. Wrens flit amongst the dense, twiggy growth of shrubs and hedges, looking for food, and in winter small flocks of redwings alight in gardens. Probably most noticeable of all are robins. They will stake out a busy gardener, darting down to pick grubs out of disturbed soil during weeding and digging.

Birds need a constant supply of water for drinking and bathing and it is important to make sure this is available, especially during drought and frost. They also like a good perimeter of trees and shrubs on which they can roost and perch, while checking out the garden to make sure it is safe to land.

If I were planning a bird-friendly border, I would choose a backbone of shrubs which reliably produce fruits they can eat. Hip-bearing roses (such as shrubby *R. moyesii* 'Geranium', shrubby *R. rugosa* types, shrub *R.* 'Penelope', climbing rose 'Etoile de Hollande', ground-cover rose 'Suffolk' and, of course, the dog rose (*R. canina*),

Pyracantha, Cotoneaster, hawthorn, elder and rowan are all suitable. Apple trees are invaluable, so include one of these as well. Dwarf trees and trained forms have become popular for smaller gardens, but the romantic appeal of a proper apple tree should not be underestimated and nor can its usefulness for birds and insects. Fill

Ponds

For any kind of garden wildlife, a pond is a marvellous asset. Ponds act as breeding grounds for yet more insects and also for frogs, which are good slug eaters. Birds, bees and other animals can drink and bathe in the water. Important considerations when building a pond are to have sloping sides, so that birds can safely hop in and out. Frogs, too, need to be able to get out easily. They must surface to breathe and a gradual slope ensures that they can do this. Shelves for marginal plants are necessary, since these provide valuable cover around the pond. Plants like water iris, forget-me-not and mint, along with monkey musk, marsh marigolds and other marginals also help shade the pond. Only half to two thirds of the surface should be shaded, cutting down the light which encourages excess algal growth, yet still admitting enough light for pond life of all sorts to thrive.

A pond can be effectively slotted into the front of a border, as long as it is netted in autumn to catch any leaves from trees growing at the back. If the pond is primarily to attract wildlife, then I would argue against introducing fish. They are pretty, but foul the water with their droppings. Unless the balance of life is very carefully maintained, algae feed on the fish effluent and proliferate, causing green, soupy water.

gaps with plants that bear lots of seed, including teasel, which though they do seed themselves around a bit, are attractive both to us and to birds.

Borders for Bees

Other visitors which really make a garden come alive are bees. Quietly going about their own business, humming and buzzing as they gather nectar and pollen, are streamlined honey bees and fat, furry bumbles. Without them we would be lost, since they are our pollinators, ensuring good sets of fruit and vegetables as well as setting seed of ornamental plants. Attracting them to a garden is not difficult, but they do have their preferences. Most honey bees are visitors from a keen bee keeper's hive. They will fly two or three miles in their quest for nectar, contributing to a fine, flavoursome honey collected from a wide variety of flowers. We tend to think of garden flowers as being their first choice, but they also love to visit trees like limes when they are in blossom.

Some bumble bees live in small communities and others are solitary. It is quite common to find a bumble bee nest in a compost heap, or perhaps in the rock garden, with the nest tucked down alongside one of the rocks. If so, it is best not to disturb them. At the end of summer, the nest will die out, with a new queen leaving to hibernate and begin a new nest elsewhere in the spring. Now and again, bees can be a nuisance because they are too fat to fit in a flower.

To get at the nectaries, they often bite through petals into the base of flowers like heathers and runner beans, bypassing the pollen and sometimes causing the flower to fall.

Solitary bumbles may make their homes by burrowing holes in banks or the soft mortar of old walls. Leaf cutter bees can be rather irritating, but are interesting. They cut oval or round pieces from the edges of leaves (particularly those of roses). With these pieces they construct tubular nests of four cells with a neat-fitting lid, slotting them down beside rocks or stones, or inside plant pots in the greenhouse. The cells are filled with chewed pollen and an egg laid in each one. Grubs eat the pollen and eventually emerge in the spring as adult bees.

To encourage bees, plan borders with a succession of their favourite flowers. This could start with *Viburnum tinus*, or laurustinus, an excellent evergreen which opens heads of white flowers all winter. Winter jasmine and Christmas roses will contribute to this season and can be followed up with spring bulbs, *Cotoneaster*, *Potentilla*, lavender and thyme. During autumn, Michaelmas daisies, ivy, *Sedum* and goldenrod are all popular.

Managing Wildlife Borders

It is important to remember that even pesticides are unlikely to give one hundred per cent control of a pest. You might just as well let nature take its course, allowing a natural equilibrium to take place between pests and their natural predators. It may be better to live comfortably with a high population of birds, insects and hedgehogs (good pest eaters) while tolerating a few blemishes on leaves and maggots in fruit.

In late spring, there is often a sudden influx of aphids, clustering on the young shoots and flower buds of roses and honeysuckle. This usually happens a good few weeks in advance of the build-up of ladybird and hoverfly populations which, later in the summer, do an admirable job of clearing aphids up by eating them voraciously. For those who cannot bear to see their favourite plants ravaged, I suggest using a product containing Pirimicarb. This selective insecticide targets aphids, yet leaves most of their natural predators unscathed. Since few of us are efficient enough to spot and treat every green and black fly, some will still remain for the ladybirds and their ilk when they do arrive.

It is both the adults and larvae of ladybirds which eat aphids. Learn to spot the larvae, which look rather like tiny lizards with legs at the front and a tail behind. The larvae of hoverflies are even more strange, like small, flat specks attached to leaves where aphids are present. Planting plenty of flat-topped, particularly yellow flowers like *Limnanthes douglasii* (poached egg plant), height 15 cm (6 in) and spread 10 cm (4 in), attracts the adult hover-flies which then lay their eggs.

There are numerous methods for defeating slugs in gardens. Surrounding vulnerable plants with barriers of coarse grit, baked egg shells, bark or soot often works, since the slugs' slimy bodies do not cross them easily. Slug 'pubs' are shallow containers buried in the ground and filled with beer. Attracted by the sticky liquid, the slugs fall in and drown. There are also slug killers on the market which are environmentally friendly. One, which is watered into the soil, contains a solution of nematodes. These microscopic, worm-like creatures, which attack slugs naturally, are put into the ground in vastly increased numbers where they enter the slugs and kill them. They remain effective for a period of six weeks.

If you do resort to slug pellets containing ingredients poisonous to birds and mammals, remember that only one pellet every 15 cm (6 in) is required. Use them really sparingly, in a ring around vulnerable plants, or in a line adjacent to a hedge or undergrowth where slugs hide during the daytime and which they would have to cross to get to the plants at night. It is only too common to see pellets scattered like a mulch with no thought for either economy or their poisonous nature.

Pheromone traps hung in apple trees during May trap male codling moths, cutting down the number of eggs layed and hence the number of maggoty apples.

Some gardeners are bothered by worm casts on lawns during autumn. Choose a dry day to brush these over the lawn. It gets rid of them and top dresses the lawn at the same time.

Fragrant Borders

~

Borders tend to be judged visually, relying on their ability to provide a satisfying contour of shapes, or perhaps a succession of beautiful flowers. Often we are so bewitched by the sight of things that we forget about our senses: sound and smell. The sounds of a border come largely from the susurrus of different leaves in the wind, especially those of eucalyptus, bamboos and grasses. There may also be the tinkling of a water feature, or footfalls on a variety of pathing materials.

Scent is different, in that it can be so varied and sometimes intense, yet when it succeeds in pleasing or astonishing garden visitors, this is rarely planned. However, it is possible to make sure that fragrant plants are included or added to borders to provide their scent at different times of the day throughout the year, in sun or shade. Choose a sheltered border to plant for perfume, so it lingers and is not wasted on the wind. Try not to mix too many different perfumes at once, aiming instead for clean, distinct fragrances. Some individual plants such as summer-flowering *Nicotiana affinis* (night-scented tobacco plant), height 75 cm (30 in) and spread 30 cm (1 ft), late winter-blooming *Daphne odora*, height and spread 1.5 m (5 ft), and summer-flowering *Philadelphus coronarius* (mock orange), height 2.5 m (8 ft) and spread 1.5 m (5 ft), are capable of scenting the air for a long distance. Others, such as rose flowers and plants with aromatic leaves, must be accessible, so that you can get close enough to smell them.

The Fragrant Border Plan

Roses prefer a hearty soil, so a well-nourished, well-drained situation would be the best choice here. Full sun will bring out the fragrances of both flowers and leaves.

Planting perfumed roses is a popular way of ensuring scent in a border. In the photograph on page 83 'Aloha', truly a modern, large-flowered climber, has been chosen to star in its alternative role as a free-standing shrub. Rose-pink petals are tightly packed in double flowers which keep up a good succession throughout summer. A versatile rose, it is happy to grow even on poor soils. Its partner in the border is the paler pink 'Fritz Nobis', a modern shrub rose which opens its clusters of double flowers just once, in early summer, with a later show of red hips.

This type of planting could be emulated on a smaller scale by choosing more diminutive perfumed roses underplanted with aromatic favourites like *Artemisia,* thyme and lavender.

Scented Roses

There are so many well-scented roses it is hard to list favourites. Among cluster-

flowered (floribunda) varieties, I like 'Anne Harkness', height 1.2 m (4 ft) and spread 60 cm (2 ft), although the apricot-yellow blooms have only a light perfume. White 'Margaret Merril', height 90 cm (3 ft) and spread 60 cm (2 ft), has a rich fragrance. 'Alec's Red', height 90 cm (3 ft) and spread 60 cm (2 ft), is a highly perfumed hybrid tea which is a delight to the nose on a warm day, when its petals are like velvet. 'Fragrant Cloud', height 75 cm (30 in) and spread 60 cm (2 ft), has good fragrance, but its coral-red

Perfume comes from two different sources in garden plants. There is the scent of flowers, here represented by roses, then there is also the perfume released from aromatic foliage when leaves are rubbed or pressed. Silvery southern-wood and apple mint make a visually and sensually satisfying underplanting.

~

Planting Guide: page 84
Border Plan: page 82

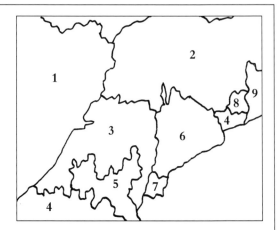

Planting Guide (see page 83)

1. *Rosa* 'Aloha', H: 3 m (10 ft), S: 1.8 m (6 ft).

2. 3 x *Rosa* 'Fritz Nobis', H: 1.5 m (5 ft),
S: 1.2 m (4 ft).

3. 2 x *Artemisia abrotanum* (lad's love,
southernwood), H and S: 75 cm (30 in).

4. *Geranium x magnificum,* H: 45 cm (18 in), S:
60 cm (2 ft).

5. *Alchemilla mollis* (lady's mantle), H and S: 45
cm (18 in).

6. 3 x *Mentha suaveolens* 'Variegata' (variegated
apple mint), H: 30–45 cm (12–18 in), S: 60 cm
(2 ft).

7. *Primula vulgaris* (primrose), H and S:
15–20 cm (6–8 in).

8. *Brachyglottis* 'Sunshine' (syn. *Senecio*
'Sunshine') H: 1–1.2 m (3–4 ft), S: 1.2–1.8 m

Plot size: length 4.5 m (15 ft); depth 2 m (7 ft)

(4–6 ft).

9. *Juniperus* x *media* 'Pfitzeriana Aurea'
(prostrate juniper), H: 90 cm (3 ft), S: 1.8 m
(6 ft).

colouring is not particularly restful to live with. 'Prima Ballerina' is a clear, rose pink. In the climbing department, my favourite is apricot-pink 'Compassion', height 3 m (10 ft) and spread 2.5 m (8 ft), but I also admire the sumptuous blooms of deep red 'Guinée' although it is not at all a good 'doer'. Milky-white 'Madame Alfred Carrière' and pink 'Madame Grégoire Staechelin' are both fine roses.

Scent for Autumn

At first, I thought there would be hardly any plants to mention for this season, when you tend to think more of leaf mould, apples in store and the fungal odour of mushrooms and toad-stools. In the tree department, there is *Cercidiphyllum japonicum* (katsura), height 15 m (50 ft) and spread 10.5 m (35 ft), grown mainly for its delightful, pink, new growth in spring as its fresh crop of circular leaves unfolds. In autumn, these same leaves smell distinctly and mouthwateringly of caramel if they are crushed when dry and brown prior to falling. A whiff of the insignificant blooms of evergreen *Elaeagnus* x *ebbingei*, height and spread 3.6 m (12 ft), can certainly turn heads, as can that from the pristine white flowers of *Hosta plantaginea,* height 60 cm (2 ft) and spread 90 cm (3 ft). Another good, perfumed border plant is a herbaceous clematis, *C. heracleifolia davidiana* 'Wyevale' which sports small, blue flowers on a plant reaching a height of 90 cm (3 ft) and a spread of 75 cm (30 in).

Scent for Winter

A surprising number of winter blooms are scented, some wafting their perfume some distance through the air. A particularly memorable group of *Hamamelis* (witch hazel) underplanted with *Sarcococca* (Christmas box) at Kew Gardens could be detected for several metres and the two made a delightfully sweet composition. In a smaller garden, the same idea could be copied, using perhaps spidery yellow-flowered *Hamamelis* x *intermedia* 'Mollis', height and spread 3.5 m (12 ft), which eventually makes a small, tree-like shape, underplanted with a group of *Sarcococca humilis*, which reaches only 60 cm (2 ft) in height and spreads to 75 cm (30 in). *Hamamelis* grow well on all but shallow, chalky soils, but must be watered during summer droughts if they are to flower well the following year.

Other winter favourites include *Viburnum* x *bodnantense* 'Dawn', a shrub which reaches a height of some 2.5 m (8 ft) with a bit of pruning. Sweetly scented, pink flowers open when the weather is mild and can continue right throughout the season. Mahonias, too, enjoy a long season of flowering. A shrub which makes one wait for its flowers is *Chimonanthus praecox* (wintersweet). Five to six years after planting, it begins to produce yellow, bell-shaped flowers which are so spicily sweet they offer instant reassurance that the wait was worthwhile. The shrub will reach a height of 2.5 m (8 ft) with a spread of 3 m (10 ft) and flowers open in late winter.

Scent for Spring

For spring, I would use as feature plants for a border a pair of *Viburnum carlesii* 'Diana', deciduous shrubs which will reach a rounded 2 m (7 ft). Deep pink buds open into heads of delightful pink flowers which have a fresh, sweet, clove-like scent to them. As underplanting, I would choose *Narcissus* 'Quail'. Smallish, bright yellow jonquil flowers are frequently several to one stem, reaching 40 cm (16 in), and the rather late flowers are sweetly scented, with a perfume which wafts across the garden.

Other plantings can include scented, white wallflowers, combined with the greenish-white flowers of the tulip 'Spring Green' for a late display. Willing to thrive in a lightly shady spot, is *Corylopsis pauciflora,* a shrub which reaches a height and spread of 1.2–1.8 m (4–6 ft); the small, pale yellow flowers have a delicate perfume. For something more substantial, yet still shade tolerant, evergreen *Osmanthus burkwoodii* bears pure white, scented blooms against its dark green foliage and can reach a rounded 3 m (10 ft). *Rhododendron luteum* is a deciduous, yellow-flowered azalea with delicious scent, reaching 1.5–2.5 m (5–8 ft) in height and spread and perfectly happy as undergrowth to deciduous trees in a woodland setting. For a delightfully almond-and-vanilla-scented, spring-flowering climber, choose evergreen, white-flowered *Clematis armandii,* height 3–5 m (10–15 ft) and spread 2–3 m (6–10 ft). Give it a sheltered south- or south-west-facing position to flourish.

Fragrant pinks like this Dianthus *'Lilian' are one of the delights of summer. Most lavenders are pleasantly scented, but this French lavender (*Lavandula stoechas *'Pedunculata') can be quite strong.*

~

Scent for Summer

Not only are there many perfumed flowers during summer, but heat is responsible for warming up the oils contained in some leaves, making aromatic foliage even more pungent than usual. An unusual deciduous shrub worth tracking down for its aromatic leaves is *Calycanthus floridus,* the Carolinan allspice. Eventually reaching a height and spread of 1.8 m (6 ft), it bears strange, deep maroonish-red flowers shaped like small magnolia blossoms. There are three outstanding aromatic evergreens for borders. Eucalyptus or gums have a clean, head-clearing smell to them and can be grown as tall trees, stooled (cut back hard every year) to form bushes of juvenile leaves, or grown as young plants for subtropical bedding. *Drimys lanceolata* (syn. *D. aromatica*), height 3.5 m (12 ft) and spread 2.5 m (8 ft), is a medium-sized beauty with shiny, deep green leaves and red stems. Do not believe anyone who says it needs full sun – plant it in a sheltered, slightly shady position and it will thrive. The aroma from crushed leaves is refreshingly spicy. Myrtles do like sun, again in a sheltered spot. My *Myrtus communis,* height and spread 1.8 m (6 ft), is planted in what I fondly call the 'Mediterranean garden', its roots treated to well-drained soil and covered with a thick mulch of shingle. The leaves are aromatic, the white, late summer flowers sweet and the seed pods spicy enough to grind up as an alternative to allspice.

Smaller aromatic shrubs are plentiful and can be mass planted for their fragrant effect. *Perovskia atriplicifolia,* known as Russian sage, creates a shimmering effect with its slender stems rising to 1–1.2 m (3–4 ft) of grey-green leaves and spires of mauve-blue flowers with a total spread of 90 cm (3 ft). This is best treated like a herbaceous perennial and will spring up from a hard cutting back each spring. A selection of lavenders is superb and just drifting your hand gently up a flower stalk is enough to release their fragrance, which varies quite surprisingly from type to type. *Santolina chamaecyparissus* (cotton lavender), height 75 cm (30 in) and spread 90 cm (3 ft) makes a lovely, low, dense bush of silvery foliage, but smells a little like cheap disinfectant.

Of the herbaceous perennials, *Monarda didyma,* known as bergamot or Oswego tea, has a delicate sweet fragrance plus the benefit of its mop-like pink or red flowers. Another worthy plant, easily raised from seed, is *Agastache foeniculum* (anise) whose leaves smell of aniseed. Mixtures will give spikes of purple, pink or white flowers which, though not particularly exciting on their own, make a soft backdrop for stronger colours. Both rise to 60–90 cm (2–3 ft) depending on soil.

Summer flower perfume is so varied and diverse there is room here to mention only favourites. In early summer, there is the soft perfume of *Wisteria* flowers, while wall shrub *Cytisus battandieri* yields up the fruity essence of pineapple. Known as pineapple or Moroccan broom, it is a super plant, bearing candles of soft, yellow, pea-like flowers against silvery, semi-evergreen foliage. Take care when siting, as plants can reach 6 m (20 ft) in height and spread unless carefully pruned. Another scent of early summer is lilac which wafts powerfully across gardens in the early evening. There are many varieties to choose, from white-flowered types to the deepest of purple. Honeysuckle, too, is a powerful wafter. Plant the early

and late Dutch honeysuckles for a summer-long fragrance trip. If there is space, try rampant semi-evergreen *Lonicera japonica,* which can reach up to 10 m (30 ft). Its perfume intensifies during evening.

Matthiola bicornis (night-scented stock), height and spread 30 cm (12 in), and *Hesperis matrionalis* (sweet rocket), height 75 cm (30 in) and spread 60 cm (2 ft), are two desirable biennials, meaning they are sown in early summer to be planted out in autumn and flower the following summer. Then there are lilies, sweet peas, the chocolate-scented *Cosmos atrosanguineus,* which achieves a height of 60 cm (2 ft) and a spread of 45 cm (18 in), and pinks, all guaranteed to delight the nose.

Herbs

Using herbs in a border will bring pleasure both in smelling the leaves and for their uses in cookery and making pot-pourri. Either group them in a terracotta pot which can be stood in the border, or design a small herb garden within the border. Alternatively, slot herbs between other plants at intervals. Bay, sage, hyssop, rosemary, fennel and oregano are good for this. Mints can be invasive, ideally restrict them by planting their roots in a bucket with drainage holes and then plunge into the soil. Do not be without *Mentha* x *piperata citrata* (eau de Cologne mint), height 30–60 cm (1–2 ft) and spread 60 cm (2 ft), which has the most amazing perfume to its leaf. Add clumps of basil as a summer annual.

Borders for Shade

～

Shady borders are usually seen as a challenge to plant and care for, yet in some ways they are a real asset to a garden. Sun-soaked borders awash with colourful flowers are all very well, but shade is restful, necessary to sit in and allows the opportunity to grow a wide range of plants which cannot tolerate full sun well.

Many shady borders are created by aspect and keen, house-hunting gardeners should pay great attention to this. Generally speaking, where the back of a house faces south, a conventional rectangular garden will receive full sun. Should it face north, the garden will be shady most of the time, but still receive reasonably good light. Where the house faces east, light will be received mainly in the morning, and if west, will be bathed in afternoon and evening light. Clearly, all this will be affected by trees, other buildings such as garages, high walls and the angle of the sun which alters throughout the year.

To choose the right plants for a border, the major concerns are whether shade is light or deep and whether soil is dry or moist. Positions of deep shade where the soil is dry can support only a restricted range of plants. As the soil becomes more moist and the shade lighter, plant choice increases dramatically.

The majority of shade-tolerant plants originate from the natural undergrowth to be found beneath the canopy of deciduous woodland trees. This includes many bulbous plants, which make their flower and leaf in spring before tree leaves unfurl, fuelling up their bulbs to lie dormant until next spring. There are autumn bulbs too, like crocus and *Colchicum*, which bloom in autumn as leaves fall and produce their own leaves in spring. Ferns and other plants tend to have lush growth which gives them large areas of leaf surface able to absorb maximum light. So much so that many cannot tolerate full sun, because they lose too much moisture from their large, plentiful leaf surfaces. Flowers are generally fewer and less showy on shade-tolerant plants, making those whose foliage can bring an occasional burst of gold, pattern of variegation, or dramatic purple tinge to a border, even more welcome.

DRY SHADE

Succeeding with dry, shaded borders can be a struggle. The majority of reliable, drought-tolerant plants need sun to thrive and most of the better shade lovers need a moist soil. Trouble spots are areas under trees, where roots rob the soil of moisture and leaves tend to act like an umbrella when it rains. Borders along the shady side of conifer hedges, whose roots suck borders dry, and also in the rain shadow of shade-casting walls are all potentially troublesome. Finding exciting plants to grow in these places is going to be difficult and even establishing a subtle mixture of rather average ground-covering plants will be a challenge.

Before planting, there are cultural ploys which will help plants establish in these difficult positions. It is all very well to say 'dig in plenty of organic matter', although liberal quantities of moisture-retentive, enriching dressings of well-rotted garden compost, manure, composted bark or mushroom compost (the last of these contains lime and therefore should not be used around lime-hating plants) will help. Sometimes, where there are lots of tree roots, it is impossible to dig anything into the ground and difficult enough to make a planting hole. Creating a slightly raised bed is often a good plan, as long as its filling of mixed soil and compost is not piled up around the trunks or stems of trees and shrubs.

Such a bed can be retained by logs, or log ends, or for a more formal setting could be made from two to three courses of bricks. I would loosen the soil beneath as much as possible first, without damaging underlying roots. Make sure it is thoroughly moist before filling in the new bed on top. This at least gives small, new plants a chance to get their roots established and will make planting them a lot easier.

When planting specimen shrubs or trees in dry shade, it is a good plan also to plant a plastic tube with one end in the root system and the other poking out of the ground. Water can be poured into

the tube and will be carried straight to the roots. Although they can tolerate dryness, watering young plants is necessary for the first couple of years until their roots are established.

The Dry Shade Border Plan

The soil type in dry shade is rarely ideal, but the plants shown in the photograph on page 90 are generally unfussy. Mulch every year in spring to improve texture and water-holding capacity.

Areas of dry shade beneath trees can almost appear lush in spring, when plants have benefited from winter rain soaking into the soil. As a ceiling of leaves develops, shadiness and dryness will increase. Although certainly not a stunning plant, *Trachystemon* is worth having for its large leaves. It belongs in the same family as borage and pentaglottis. Keep an eye on it as, like *Pentaglottis,* it can become a bit of a thug unless restricted now and again. Pretty blue flowers appear low down just as foliage grows up in spring.

While *Trachystemon* is well known for its general tenacity, the other dominant plant here is usually described as one liking moist soils. The mass of pink flowers belongs to *Dicentra formosa,* of which there are several good varieties. In my garden I grow *D.* 'Stuart Boothman', height 45 cm (18 in) and spread 30 cm (1 ft), which has beautiful, grey-green leaves and pink flowers which open throughout spring, but also gives a second flush at the end of summer. My

Varying leaf shapes and textures combine with the flowers of Dicentra *and* Polgonatum *to make an interesting underplanting for this flowering cherry.*

~

Planting Guide: page 91
Border Plan: page 89

the plants knit well together without too much competition. Simply use greater or lesser numbers as needed to fill the space. Within two years, my single *Dicentra* 'Stuart Boothman' was able to be divided into 50 root sections, all of which took.

plants have performed really well in a dry soil, but their rather fleshy mats of roots have been treated to plenty of organic matter.

In dry shade, using bold blocks of plants is effective and when they succeed

Shrubs for Dry Shade

Specimen evergreen shrubs suitable for dry shade include *Aucuba japonica*, the spotted laurel, which will reach a height and spread of some 3 m (10 ft). To

Planting Guide (see page 90)

1. 25 x *Dicentra formosa*, H and S: 30 cm (1 ft).

2. 5 x *Anchusa azurea*, H and S: 50 cm (20 in).

3. 5 x *Trachystemon orientalis*, H: 60 cm (24 in), S: 75 cm (30 in).

4. *Prunus* 'Shirofugen' (flowering cherry), H and S: 7.5 m (25 ft).

5. 3 x *Polygonatum* x *hybridum* (Solomon's seal), H: 90 cm (3 ft), S: 30 cm (1 ft)

Plot size: length 3.5 m (12 ft); depth 2.75 m (9 ft)

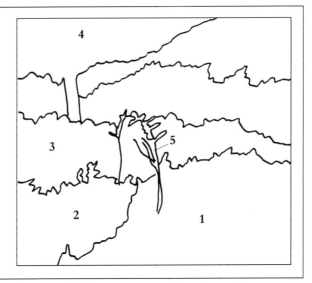

bright up the gloom, choose a bright-leaved variety like *A. j.* 'Crotonifolia' or 'Picturata'. *Prunus laurocerasus* 'Otto Luyken' is good too. A narrow-leaved cherry laurel, it will reach a height of 90 cm (3 ft) and spread of 1.5 m (5 ft). Spikes of small, white flowers open in late spring. Another spring flowerer is *Mahonia aquifolium*, the Oregon grape, height also 90 cm (3 ft), and spread 1.5 m (5 ft). Bunches of fragrant, yellow flowers are honey-scented and followed by blue-black fruits. Some leaves turn a lovely red during winter. There are many *Cotoneasters* to try, too, though possibly not in the densest of shade. Evergeens include *C. franchetii* (orange-red fruit), height and spread 3 m (10 ft), *C.* 'Rothschildianus' (yellow berries), height and spread 5 m (15 ft), and *C. salicifolius* (red fruits), height and spread 5 m (15 ft).

Smaller shrubs could include varieties of *Euonymus fortunei*, which vary in height from 60 cm (2 ft) to 2.5 m (8 ft),

Sarcococca (Christmas box) and *Ruscus* (butcher's broom). Also the rather unusual *Rubus odoratus* (flowering raspberry or thimbleberry), height and spread 2.5 m (8 ft), is worth cultivating for its large, velvety, lobed leaves and peeling, thornless stems, although its fruits are sadly unpalatable. Cut back every year in spring to keep growth under control. *Pachysandra terminalis*, height 30 cm (1 ft) and spread 45 cm (18 in), and *Hypericum calycinum* (rose of Sharon), height 25 cm (10 in) and spread 1.5 m (5 ft), are sub-shrubby stalwarts of dry, shady areas.

Smaller Plants for Dry Shade

Geranium macrorrhizum, which grows to 30 cm (12 in) in height with a spread of 60 cm (2 ft), produces mounds of neat, aromatic leaves and pretty, pink flowers in early summer and is just one of the hardy geraniums which will tolerate dry shade.

Its foliage is semi-evergreen and becomes tinged with red in autumn. *Bergenia* 'Mrs Crawford' (elephant's ears), *Iris foetedissima* (the stinking iris, grown for its showy orange-red fruit in winter), height 30–90 cm (1–3 ft) and spread indefinite, small varieties of dead nettle such as *Lamium* 'White Nancy', height 15 cm (6 in) and spread 20–30 cm (8–12 in), and indispensable, marbled-leaved *Arum italicum* 'Pictum', height 15–25 cm (6–10 in) and spread 20–30 cm (8–12 in), are all good.

Add to the list *Polystichum setiferum* (soft shield fern), height 60 cm (2 ft) and spread 45 cm (18 in), and an interesting plant called *Liriope muscari* (lilyturf), height 30 cm (1 ft) and spread 45 cm (18 in). Tufts of long, narrow leaves are joined by spikes of small, bobbly, violet flowers in autumn. Varieties with gold edges to their leaves show up well in the shade.

Some of the most successful bulbs include hardy cyclamen, especially autumn-flowering *C. hederifolium,* height to 10 cm (4 in) and spread 10–15 cm (4–6 in), and spring-flowering *C. coum,* height to 10 cm (4 in) and spread 5–10 cm (2–4 in), *Eranthis hyemalis* (winter aconite), height 5–10 cm (2–4 in) and spread 8–10 cm (3–4 in), *Galanthus* (snowdrop), *Anemone nemorosa* (wood anemone), height 15 cm (6 in) and spread 30 cm (1 ft), bluebells and *Chionodoxa* (glory of the snow). I would also try a lovely, unusual rhizomatous plant which will spread into small clumps. *Uvularia grandiflora* (merry bells), height 45–60 cm (18–24 in) and spread 30 cm (12 in), thrives in the shade of my magnolia tree, producing its arching stems of downward-looking, yellow flowers in spring.

MOIST SHADE

Where shade is combined with a moist soil, the fun really begins. There are so many plants which enjoy these conditions, that beautiful effects can be created. So lush and architectural are some of these plants that gardeners sometimes create special borders for them where the soil is naturally dry. It is possible to excavate a wide area, line the base with a flexible pond liner, which is then punctured for drainage and filled in again to create a bog garden where moist shade lovers like *Ligularia, Hosta, Astilbe* and others will thrive. They will still need to be given water during droughts, but the liner will prevent a lot of it from seeping away, making maintenance much easier.

Most shady borders where the soil is continually enriched with added mulches of well-rotted organic matter will play host to a satisfying range of plants without the need for a pond liner, or a lot of irrigation. As long as there is no rain shadow and an absence of hungry tree roots, the fact that sun has little chance of stressing the plants means that even during dry periods they will stay fresh. At the first signs of wilting, give the border a really good soak during the evening.

I have a few shady corners and borders in my own garden. One is tucked behind a pergola which follows the sweep of a path, making a tunnel of roses, honey-suckle and clematis. An awkward corner is filled by the tall shrub *Staphylea pinnata* (bladder nut), height and spread 6 m (20 ft), but the area around this has been colonized by fairly large plants which still make their presence felt, despite competition from the fragrant pergola. My favourite is *Aruncus dioicus* (syn. *A. sylvester*), often called goat's beard. Graceful leaflets clothe stems which bear terminal, branching plumes of creamy-white flowers capable of reaching up to 1.8 m (6 ft) with a spread of 1.2 m (4 ft). Young plants need watering to establish, but once large clumps have formed, they become more self-sufficient.

The other dominant plant is *Scrophularia aquatica* 'Variegata', the varie-gated form of water figwort. Ignore books which say you should cut off developing flower stems to preserve the rosette of cream-and-green-variegated leaves. The best part is when the stems rise up to produce spikes of little, hooded, maroon flowers. They can reach a height of some 90 cm (3 ft) with a spread of 45 cm (1½ ft) in moist condi-tons. The cream-and-maroon theme is continued by plantings of *Astrantia* (mas-terwort) varieties and a ground covering of *Convallaria majalis* (lily of the valley), height 15 cm (6 in) and spread indefinite, which release their glorious, sweet per-fume in late spring.

To one side, though, is an interwoven mass of fern fronds from the virtually evergreen *Polystichum setiferum* (soft shield fern), height 60 cm (2 ft) and spread 45 cm (18 in), which grows in moist or dry shade, and *Dicentra spectabilis* (bleeding heart or Dutchman's trousers), whose arching sprays of pendent, heart-shaped pink-and-white flowers rise up to 75 cm (30 in) and achieve a spread of 50 cm (20 in) in spring. *Polystichum setiferum* is easy to propagate by removing fronds covered with small plantlets, or bulbils. These, gently pushed into the sur-face of moist potting compost, will root and grow into individual plants which can be planted in an effective group.

Very Damp Areas

There is a tendency among gardeners to view any extreme soil condition as a problem to be solved. In fact, there will always be a range of plants which have adapted to survive these extremes. Choose from these and the plants should settle in well. I was once asked to plant a border where the water table was high and the ground periodically flooded by an adjacent river. On excavating what looked like a mound, I found that some previous owner had attempted to raise their plants above the flood by building a rather poor rock garden. Subsequent and repeated floods had gradually submerged the rocks and plants with silt, which sup-ported a thriving weed population. The obvious answer to this moist border with its dappled shade was to convert it into a natural bog garden.

The royal fern *Osmunda regalis* and water irises were used along the bank, while the soil, once weeded and levelled,

Moist shade enables a wide variety of plants to knit together, blending many shades of green with variegated and purple foliage. When planning a shade border, it is foliage that takes centre stage and flowers are an added bonus.

～

Planting Guide: page 96
Border Plan: page 96

was planted with stately *Rheum palmatum* 'Atrosanguineum' which reaches a height and spread of 1.8 m (6 ft). Spectacular in bloom, this ornamental rhubarb bears glowing red purple leaves when young and unfolding. In summer, stems bearing feathery panicles of small crimson flowers rise above the beautifully cut foliage. A group of *Darmera peltata* (*Peltiphyllum*

peltatum) was planted for the heads of pink flowers produced in spring on long stalks before the foliage appears. These large, rounded leaves take over, reaching up to 1–1.2 m (3–4 ft) and are tinged with a lovely russet red before dying off in the autumn. Smaller plants like *Primula florindae* (bog primula),, height 60–90 cm (2–3 ft) and spread 30–60 cm (1–2 ft), the yellow flowered giant cowslip and *P. bulleyana,* height 60 cm (2 ft) and spread 30 cm (1 ft), the pink candelabra primula added colour in early summer.

Where the soil is continuously moist, plants like *Ligularia* grow lush and impressive. *L. desdemona* can reach up to 1.2 m (4 ft), with a marvellous show of dark-rounded to heart-shaped leaves joined by incredible, shaggy-petalled, orange flowers which spread to 60 cm (2 ft) in summer. *L.* 'The Rocket' can reach 1–1.8 m (3–6 ft) and bears spikes of yellow flowers rising above almost triangular leaves. *Rodgersia*, too, give of their best where soil is moist. *R. pinnata, R. podophylla* and

It is the shape, texture and colour of leaves that make successful plantings in moist, shady borders. Here fern fronds blend with Ligularia, Hosta fortunei *'Gold Standard' and* Hellebore, *with contrast added in the form of a terracotta urn.*

~

Planting Guide (see page 94)

1. 2 x *Juniperus* x *media* 'Pfitzeriana' (pros
trate juniper), H: 90 cm (3 ft), S: 1.5 m (5 ft).

2. *Euonymus fortunei* 'Emerald and Gold', H:
60 cm (2 ft), S: 75 cm (30 in).

3. Ground cover such as *Euonymus fortunei
radicans*, H and S: 90 cm (3 ft) with pruning.

4. 5 x *Heuchera* 'Palace Purple', H and S: 45
cm (18 in).

5. Hosta such as *H. sieboldiana* 'Frances
Williams', H and S: 90 cm (3 ft).

6. 4 x *Lamium maculatum* (deadnettle) such as
'White Nancy', H: 20 cm (8 in), S: 60 cm (2 ft).

7. 3 x *Phalaris arundinacea* var. *picta* (gardener's
garters), H and S: 90 cm (3 ft).

8. *Juniperus* x *media* 'Pfitzeriana Aurea' (golden
prostrate juniper), H: 90 cm (3 ft), S: 1.5 m
(5 ft).

9. 7 x Pale pink astilbe such as *A.* 'Sprite',
H and S: 45 cm (18 in).

10. 6 x Ground cover of *Lamium galeobdolon*,
H: 30 cm (1 ft), S: indefinite, and 6 x *Brunnera*

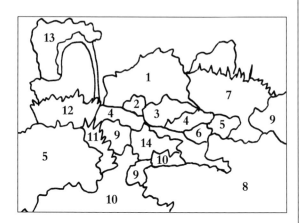

Plot size: length 5.5 m (18 ft); depth 2.5 m (8 ft)

macrophylla, H: 45 cm (18 in), S: 60 cm (2 ft).

11. 2 x *Iris pseudacorus* 'Variegata' (variegated
yellow flag), H: 1.8 m (6 ft), S: indefinite.

12. 3 x *Iris ensata* (syn. *I. kaempferi*), H: 75 cm
(30 in), S: indefinite.

13. White rose, climber such as 'Iceberg', H:
2.75 m (9 ft), S: 1.8 m (6 ft).

14. *Astilbe* such as A. 'Fanal', H and S: 60 cm
(2 ft).

R. aesculifolia all have imposing leaves rather reminiscent of horse chestnut and bear sprays of pink or cream flowers in summer. They can reach a height of some 1.2 m (4 ft) and a spread of 75 cm (2.5 ft). The leaves of the slightly shorter *R. tabularis* are rather like round umbrellas.

The Moist Shade Border Plan

The interesting thing about the planting in this border, shown in the photograph on page 94, is the use of different shapes and colours of foliage. There are the dense masses created by the needles of prostrate junipers, next to bright, evergreen *Euonymus*, silver-splashed *Lamium* and the airy, waving stems of *Phalaris*. Boldness is represented by the purple *Heuchera* and *Hosta* leaves, while the vertical spears of iris are a complete contrast. Feathery dark and pale pink *Astilbe* flowers team well with the exotic purple blooms of *Iris ensata* to create just enough colour to complete the picture.

Although these twin borders are large, similar ground-covering plantings could work equally well on a smaller scale. In that case, miss out on rampant types like *Lamium* and large, spreading junipers.

Collectable shade lovers

A shady border where the soil is not particularly boggy, but receives an ordinary amount of water, can make a lovely home for two very collectable types of plants. There are many beautiful, yet undemanding hardy ferns which can create a decidedly Victorian atmosphere. Team them up with *Pulmonaria* (lungwort) which is a popular plant for either dry or moist shade. Among the ferns, I like dainty *Athyrium filix-femina* (lady fern), height up to 90 cm (3 ft) and spread to 75 cm (2½ ft), and its varieties.

During the Victorian fern craze, collectors scoured the countryside for interesting variants of our native ferns, with the result that there are many named varieties to look out for. One of the strangest is *A. f.* 'Frizelliae' which more resembles parsley than an ordinary lady fern. *Asplenium scolopendrium,* the heart's tongue fern, with a height and spread of 30 cm (1 ft), also has some fascinating varieties with undulating fronds or those with complicated cristate ends. However, *Matteuccia struthiopteris,* the shuttlecock fern or ostrich feather fern, is hard to beat. The fronds unfurl grace-fully in spring, making shapes that exactly resemble fresh, green shuttle-cocks. Mature ferns reach some 90 cm (3 ft) tall with a spread of up to 45 cm (1½ ft) and one plant sends up small replicas of itself on stolons, to form attractive colonies.

Pulmonaria is a superb plant which bear early spring flowers close to the ground. These open pink, in *P. saccharata,* height 30 cm (1 ft) and spread 60 cm (2 ft), but turn blue as they age so that both colours are present at once. As flowers start to open, new leaves begin to grow, revealing their silver spots as they age. There are now many varieties, some with plain pink, blue or white flowers, with soft green leaves or foliage heavily marked with silvery white. One very good example is an exceptionally spotty variety called 'Leopard'.

An interesting shade-lover for the front of a border is *Asarum europaeum.* The chief feature of this woodland plant is its glossy, evergreen, kidney-shaped leaves to 15 cm (6 in) which completely hide rather in-conspicuous, but nevertheless interesting, brown, spring flowers. Similarly named *Arisarum proboscideum* is the mouse-tail plant much loved by children. In spring, arrow-shaped leaves spring up to 10 cm (4 in), almost concealing little, hooded flowers with long, brown spathes which sweep up to 15 cm (6 in) long tails.

Flower Arranger's Borders

~

Keen flower arrangers are fascinating to watch, as they can perform magic with a pile of foliage and one or two perfect blooms. In order to pursue their art, they need as wide a palette as possible of suitable leaves and stems, as well as masses of small, frothy flowers such as lady's mantle, *Bupleurum* or *Gypsophila*. Impressive floral displays seem to owe as much to a backing of foliage as to the flowers themselves. There are so many exciting colours and textures in leaves and fronds, from the sword-shaped, spiky leaves of iris and New Zealand flax *(Phormium tenax)*, through rounded hosta leaves to the shimmering effect of beech, or cool, feathery fern fronds. *Hypericum* and even raspberry shoots have become popular for natural, cottage-style effects.

Where the whole garden is to be used as a resource for arranging, this should be reflected in the trees and shrubs selected to make the backbone of the garden, through smaller shrubs and herbaceous perennials, to annuals and bulbs. While thinking of shapes and colours for the garden, plus filling vases at all times of year, try not to loose sight of matching the right plants to soil and aspect.

~

Planting Guide: page 100
Border Plan: page 100

Planting Guide (see page 98)

1. *Eucalyptus globulus* (blue gum),
H and S: 1.8 m (6 ft) as a stooled plant.

2. Purple form of *Cotinus coggygria*
(smoke bush), such as *C. c.* 'Notcutts
Variety', H and S: 3.5 m (12 ft).

3. 3 x Pink-flowered *Astrantia*
(masterwort) such as *A. major* 'Rosea',
H: 60 cm (2 ft), S: 45 cm (18 in).

4. *Rodgersia pinnata* 'Superba',
H: 90 cm (3 ft), S: 75 cm (30 in).

5. *E. fortunei* 'Emerald Gaiety',
H: 90 cm (3 ft) S: 1.5 m (5 ft).

6. Small shrub such as *Viburnum plicatum*
'Nanum Semperflorens' (dwarf
Japanese snowball tree) H: 2 m (6 ft) S: 1.5
m (5 ft)

7. *Parahebe perfoliata* (digger's speedwell) H and S:
45 cm (18 in).

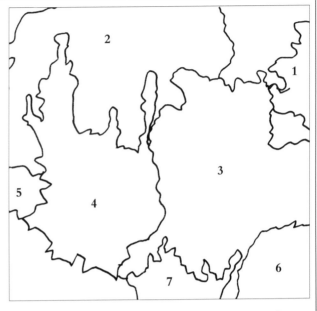

Plot size: length 2.5 m (8 ft); depth 1.8 m (6 ft)

A garden can provide a lot of the material a flower arranger requires, offering plenty of variety and great savings on what needs to be bought in. When planning a border for flower arranging, the two main considerations are colour co-ordination and all-year-round interest. There is a third, and that is quality. What will make your arrangements stand out from the ordinary is that little bit of extra care and attention in seeking out the best and most unusual varieties on offer.

Flower Arranger's Border Plan

The soil should be rich and moisture-retentive enough to persuade a good performance out of the *Rodgersia* and *Astrantia*, yet well-drained and not water-logged. These will do best in a sunny or semi-shaded position.

Our flower arranger's border pictured on pages 98-9 not only offers a good range of shrubs and herbaceous perennials for cutting, but also contains some exciting shades of purple, pink and silver which combine as well in the garden as they might in a vase.

This idea can be continued around the garden, matching plants together so that they blend and contrast, offering inspiration throughout the seasons. Such a perfect tapestry is unlikely to be achieved overnight, so be prepared for continual evaluation and be willing to move key plants around while still young until they find the right partners.

The feature plants used here are a dramatic, purple-leaved *Cotinus* (smoke bush) and silvery *Eucalyptus*. Gum trees, despite their antipodean origins, can make reliable garden specimens. They will grow into tall trees if left to their own devices, but can be cut back hard every spring, which makes them bush out into a more shrubby habit. This stooling consists of cutting or sawing the main stem almost to ground level. Several stems will be produced as a result and all of these should be cut back every spring. The result of this is not only reduction in height, with all the material within arm's reach, but juvenile foliage is maintained. Young *Eucalyptus* leaves are more rounded in shape and a brighter, fresher colour than more mature foliage. *E. gunnii* (the cider gum), height 30 m (100 ft) and spread 22.5 m (75 ft), is most commonly grown, but *E. glaucescens* (Tingirini gum), height 12 m (40 ft) and spread 7.5 m (25 ft), *E. perriniana* (spinning gum), height and spread 9 m (30 ft), and *E. niphophila* (snow gum), height and spread 15 m (50 ft), are also worth a try and are easy to raise from spring-sown seed.

Against this backdrop, the key perennials make interesting outlines. Both of these perform well in semi-shade and bear useful sprays of flowers. Masterwort *(Astrantia major)* is a well-tempered perennial in *Umbelliferae*, the same family as carrot and cow parsley. On closer inspection, it can be seen that the blooms are actually heads of small flowers surrounded by papery bracts, each about 2.5 cm (1 in) across. Although here they are pale pink, there are greenish-white and deep pink, almost red types. In common with other perennials whose flowers tend to rise up above a mound of leaves, they have the added bonus of not needing to be staked and tied. The same should be true of *Rodgersia*. Interesting, horse chestnut-shaped foliage is joined by spires of pink flowers in summer. This plant likes a moisture-retentive soil, so mulch heavily over the roots in spring while the soil is moist. On thin, sandy soils, it will need to be watered regularly if not grown in a specially constructed bog garden.

Usefully covering the ground in the far left of the picture is *Euonymus fortunei* 'Emerald Gaiety', height 90 cm (3 ft) and spread 1.5 m (5 ft). There are several variegated forms of *E. fortunei* which make mounds of evergreen foliage. Not only are they excellent evergreen, weed-smothering gap-fillers, but their foliage is also useful for arrangements at any time of the year.

Colour Themes

Colour theming the garden is a fun idea, but as well as grouping colours together, think about how to run one into the next as well as making a few dramatic contrasts. Garden design and floral art have a lot in common. The following are flower arranger's favourites that you might like to include.

Yellow, Cream and White
Corylus avellana 'Contorta' (twisted nut). Produces interesting, twisted stems hung with creamy catkins in spring. H and S: 3 m (10 ft), or more if unpruned.

Jasminum nudiflorum (winter jasmine). Easy and reliable, this jasmine should be trained against a fence or wall. Bare stems burst into yellow flowers during winter. H and S: 3 m (10 ft).

Philadelphus 'Belle Etoile' (mock orange). This is a middle-sized shrub whose lovely, fragrant, white blooms are marked with maroon. H: 2.5 m (8 ft) S: 1.8 m (6 ft).

Clematis tangutica. Ideal for pergolas and trellis, this climber produces lantern-like, yellow flowers in late summer, followed by marvellous, fluffy seed heads. H: 5 m (16 ft), S: 3 m (10 ft).

Rosa 'Iceberg' is such a good performer. White blooms open from June into autumn. Grow as a bush or climber. H: 90 cm (3 ft) S: 75 cm (30 in).

Chrysanthemum x *superbum* 'Wirral Supreme' (Shasta daisy) is a herbaceous perennial whose double, white blooms with yellow centres open in July. H: 75 cm (30 in) S: 60 cm (2 ft).

Rudbeckia fulgida 'Goldsturm' is a herbaceous perennial with dark-centred, yellow, daisy-like blooms, H: 75 cm (30 in) S: 45 cm (18 in).

Gypsophila paniculata 'Bristol Fairy' (baby's breath) is a herbaceous perennial which, given a well-drained soil, will grow well and make a haze of small, white flowers. H and S: 60–75 cm (24–30 in).

Hosta fortunei 'Aureomarginata' and most other hostas are invaluable for their structured foliage. This one has creamy margins to its mid-green leaves. H: 60 cm (2 ft).

Blue, Silver and Grey
Elaeagnus ebbingei is an evergreen shrub with silvery leaves and inconspicuous, but sweetly fragrant, late summer flowers. H and S: 2 m (7 ft), more if unpruned.

Syringa vulgaris 'Blue Hyacinth' is a lovely lilac, producing scented, pale lilac blooms in late spring. H: 3 m (10 ft) S: 2.75 m (9ft).

Hedera helix 'Glacier' has a silvery edge to its green leaves. All ivies are lovely for their trailing stems. H: 3 m (10 ft).

Agapanthus Headbourne Hybrids produce superb heads of blue flowers in summer, H: 90 cm (3 ft), S: 60 cm (2 ft).

Convolvulus cneorum is a small, sun-loving evergreen with soft, silvery leaves and saucer-shaped, white flowers in summer, H and S: 75 cm (30 in).

Stachys byzantina (lamb's tongue or lamb's ears) has soft, silvery leaves. Spikes of small, pink flowers rise up in summer. H and S: 60 cm (2ft).

Nigella damascena (love-in-a-mist) is a pretty annual which can be direct sown into the ground. Even the seed pods are attractive. H: 60 cm (2ft), S: 20 cm (8 in).

Lathyrus 'Cambridge Blue' (sweet pea) is a lovely pale blue with superb fragrance. Sow in autumn or spring and train up trellis, a wigwam of canes or garden shrubs, H: 2.5 m (8 ft).

Purple and Pink
Pittosporum tenuifolium 'Tom Thumb' is one of the hardiest pittosporums. In winter, the foliage turns rich purple on a small, rounded bush. H and S: 1–2 m (3–6 ft).

Rosa glauca is a lovely species with grey-purple foliage, red stems and single, white-centred, pink flowers. H: 1.8 m (6ft), S: 1.5 m (5 ft).

Rosa 'New Dawn' is a useful, soft pink climbing rose. Flowers are borne in clusters from summer to autumn. H and S: 3 m (10 ft).

Nerine bowdenii boasts superb stems of pink, lily-like blooms which rise naked from the soil in autumn, just when fresh flowers are most needed. H: 60 cm (2 ft), S: 15cm (6 in).

x *Heucherella tiarelloides* is an ever-green ground-cover plant which bears spikes of small, bell-shaped, pink flowers in early summer. H and S: 45 cm (18 in).

Acanthus spinosus (bear's breeches) has striking, architectural foliage, plus tall spikes of mauve-and-white flowers. H: 1.2 m (4 ft), S: 60 cm (2 ft).

Aster novae-angliae 'Harrington's Pink' is a mildew-resistant type of Michaelmas daisy with pink flowers in autumn, H: 1.2 m (4 ft), S: 60 cm (2 ft).

Astilbe 'Bressingham Beauty' is attractive in leaf and when it produces feathery, pink flower sprays in summer. H and S: 75 cm (30in).

Red and Orange

Ilex aquifolium 'Handsworth New Silver' is a handsome holly with purple stems, creamy leaf margins and, when pollinated by a male variety, lots of red berries in winter. H: 3.5 m (12 ft), S: 2.5 m (8 ft).

Salix alba vitellina 'Britzensis' is willow grown for its winter stems, which are a glowing orange. Cut down hard in March to maintain this fresh colour.

Plants grown specifically for cutting and drying will brighten up the garden as well. Direct-sow Helichrysum *'Bright Bikini Mixed' into gaps in vegetable or flower borders for a patch of glowing colour.*

103

H: 1.8 m (6 ft), S: 1.5 m (5 ft).

Cotoneaster franchetii bears arching stems of rounded leaves joined by masses of orange-red berries in autumn. H and S: 3 m (10 ft).

Rosa rugosa and other roses can be chosen for their lovely, autumnal hips which blend so well with the colours of the season. H and S: 1.8 m (6 ft).

Physalis alkekengi (Chinese lanterns) are herbaceous perennials which don't look much until their marvellous, orange seed pods set in autumn. H: 45 cm (18 in), S: 60 cm (2 ft).

Calendula (pot marigold) is an annual available in a range of warm shades. Try 'Touch of Red Mixed'. H and S: 45 cm (18 in).

Tithonia rotundifolia 'Torch' is a tall half-hardy annual which bears orange-red, dahlia-like blooms. H: 1.2 m (4 ft), S: 90 cm (3 ft).

Gardeners' Posies

Although I appreciate the skills of flower arranging, I have never managed to motivate myself sufficiently to learn any of its disciplines properly. But in common with many other gardeners, I enjoy having small bunches of garden flowers in the house. Each posy, picked in its season, makes a living reminder of what is in flower outside. This way, when I'm writing, I can admire and smell seasonal flowers and, on days when the weather is unsuitable for gardening, not miss out on favourite flowers when they're in bloom.

Gathering garden posies usually starts with clipping one or two favourite flowers, then adding more blooms and foliage. In February, a miniature vase of tiny, exquisite snowdrops and scillas can be mixed with ivy and the strange, greenish, scented flowers of *Daphne laureola,* height 90 cm (3 ft) and spread 1.5 m (5 ft). Later, it's the turn of dwarf *Narcissus*, primroses and *Pulmonaria*. In summer, fragrant roses like the rather sparsely flowered, red climber 'Guinée' are irresistible and combine with honeysuckle, the drumsticks of hybrid thrifts and lavender. A month later sweet peas, hardy annuals, *Allium sphaerocephalon*, height to 60 cm (2 ft) and spread 8–10 cm (3–4 in), and silvery *Dorycnium hirsutum*, height and spread to 60 cm (2 ft), look superb. You can please yourself whether colours tone beautifully or clash riotously.

Autumnal pickings in my garden might include the domed heads of ice plant, yellow daisies of tall *Heliopsis,* silvery *Artemisia* and the first delicately coloured rose hips off the dog rose hedge. Winter is a real challenge, but in a well-planned garden, you'll soon have a fistful of marbled leaves of *Arum italicum* 'Pictum', height 15–25 cm (6–10 in) and spread 20–30 cm (8–12 in), surrounding sprigs of scented, pink-flowered *Viburnum* x *bodnantense* 'Dawn', height 3 m (10 ft) and spread 1.8 m (6 ft), spidery witch hazel, white heather and the foliage of the delicate evergreen *Drimys aromatica.* Or promising buds of mid-winter *Iris unguicularis* with the bright foliage of evergreens like *Rhamnus alaternus* 'Argenteomarginatus', height and spread 3 m (10 ft).

Dry Borders

~

There is no escaping the fact that we frequently experience long summer droughts and that in some parts of the country particularly, we are asked to be economical with our water supplies. Artificial watering is no substitute for a good fall of rain and is not only time-consuming, but becomes difficult, if not unethical, when shortages apply.

The best way of dealing with drought is to avoid the problem. To do this it helps to understand soil type, carry out good cultivation techniques and, if necessary, change the plants. I have had to do all three in my own garden.

Those toiling with a heavy clay soil, which turns solid in winter and brick-like in summer, can actually think themselves lucky. There may be only brief periods during spring and autumn when they become workable enough to dig, but clay soils can be gradually improved by additions of copious quantities of well-rotted organic matter and sharp sand or grit. Eventually the texture will improve so that the top layer is workable during more of the year, resulting in a well nourished soil fortified with moisture and nourishment. Once plants have established in an enriched clay soil, they grow well, quickly putting their roots down to establish themselves.

On a poor, light, sandy soil, well-rotted manure or compost can be dug in by the truck load, yet it seems to disappear as fast as it is added. Mulches are slightly more successful, but they must be added thickly when the soil is moist. Water drains so quickly through the soil that in borders which are also prone to the baking effect of sun in a south- or west-facing position, it is better to choose plants more carefully to withstand drought.

The Dry Border Plan

The feature plant in the border pictured on page 106 is a well-chosen Spanish broom, which bears bright yellow, pea-like flowers in early summer. As leaves are the organs through which plants lose moisture, this stalwart example has virtually dispensed with them. Instead it relies upon a mass of bright green shoots which make an attractive feature even during winter. It is possible to reduce ultimate height and spread by trimming shoots back in early spring. The severity of such leaflessness is ameliorated by a nearby planting of wispy *Stipa tenuissima*, whose fleecy seed heads persist well into autumn and winter.

Yuccas offer year-round structure and can be relied on to tolerate long, dry periods, as can wiry-stemmed *Verbena bonariensis*. Easily raised from seed, this tall perennial should prove hardy in all but the coldest of areas, especially when planted in well-drained soil. Should plants fail, simply raise more from a spring sowing.

This mixture of feathery stipa and mauve verbena with silver and yellow touches shows how exciting drought-tolerant plants can be

~

Planting Guide: page 107
Border Plan: page 105

With the mainstays of the border established, finishing touches should be easy to insert. Silvery artemisia and soft-leaved ballota blend well with the purple of verbena and agastache A foreground of *Allium christophii* adds large, round heads of purple flowers, followed by parchment-coloured seed heads, while lilies rise above it all with an easy grace. The reassuring quality of such borders is that when mulched with shingle, they look good even while establishing. On reaching maturity, should one or two plants succumb, the shingle-filled gaps they leave are positively attractive and do not make eyesores while waiting to be filled.

When planning a deep border, it is fun to mark out areas where the mulch of gravel or shingle will be left bare to make an informal path. This can weave through the border, enabling plants to be examined more closely and allowing more low-growing plants to be used.

Drought-tolerant plants are often ground-hugging, with divided, silvery leaves, and can be waxy or covered in small hairs. All these modifications are

Planting Guide (see page 106)

1. *Spartium junceum* (Spanish broom), H and S: 3 m (10 ft).

2. 5 x *Verbena bonariensis,* H: 1.5 m (5 ft), S: 60 cm (2 ft).

3. *Yucca filamentosa* (Adam's needle), H: 1.8 m (6 ft) S: 1.5 m (5 ft).

4. 9 x *Lilium candidum*, H: 1–2 m (3–6 ft), S: 30cm (1 ft)

5. 5 x *Stipa tenuissima* (feather grass), H and S: 60 cm (2 ft).

6. 2 x *Anthemis tinctoria* 'E.C. Buxton', H and S: 75 cm (30 in).

7. Lavender such as *L. angustifolia* 'Royal Purple', H and S: 60 cm (2 ft).

8. *Ballota acetabulosa*, H: 45 cm (18 in), S: 60 cm (2 ft).

9. *Papaver rhoeas* (Shirley poppy) H: 60 cm (2 ft) S: 30 cm (1 ft) (seed).

10. 3 x *Agastache mexicana* (Mexican giant hyssop) H and S: 60 cm (2 ft).

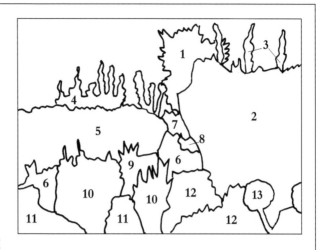

Plot size: length 3.5 m (12 ft); depth 2.75 m (9 ft)

11. 3 x *Artemisia* 'Powis Castle' (wormwood), H: 75 cm (30 in), S: 45 cm (18 in).

12 5 x *Lavandula stoechas* (French lavender), H: 60 cm (2 ft), S: 45 cm (18 in).

13 3 x *Allium christophii*, H: 30 cm (12 in), S: 20 cm (8 in).

aimed at cutting down loss of moisture. A successfully drought-tolerant plant will avoid placing vulnerable leaves in the passage of drying winds. The pores on leaves tend to be fewer and carefully protected. Some, like the sedums, have fleshy leaves capable of storing moisture. Others grow from storage organs like bulbs, corms and tubers, which can swell during rainy periods to store moisture for droughts.

Creating a Dry Border

Trees, fences and hedges also have a part to play in robbing soil of moisture. I have a west-facing border in my garden, backed by a fence with a young conifer hedge on the other side (which replaced an earlier row of thirsty elm suckers). Having tried and failed with all kinds of plants, which either looked miserable and refused to grow, or died, the obvious solution was a dry border. This, born of necessity, has turned out to be one of the most enjoyable parts of the garden.

The first task was to mark the contours of this new border on the turf. This was then cut with a half-moon and the border single-dug, with the turf skimmed off and buried face down in the bottom of each well-forked trench. The freshly dug border was then left to settle for a while, before being trodden down and raked prior to planting. This was an exciting undertaking, with drought-tolerant, sun-lovers like *Abutilon* x *suntense,* height 4.5 m (15 ft) and spread 3 m (10 ft), and hardy, high-altitude *Acacia subalpina* (mimosa), height 6 m (20 ft) and spread 4.2 m (14 ft), chosen to tie into the fence. Either side of the *Abutilon,* the blue-and-white-flowered potato vines *Solanum crispum* 'Glasnevin', height up to 6 m (20 ft), and *S. jasminoides* 'Album', height also up to 6 m (20 ft), were planted. Elsewhere, passion flower and evergreen, scented *Trachelospermum jasminoides* (star jasmine) will scramble with profusion to reach a height of up to 2.4 m (8 ft). All will have to be trained and pruned to restrict size

The beauty of a well-drained border protected by a fence is that unusual tender plants stand more of a chance of lasting through the winter. Their worst enemies are wet, cold soils and exposed positions. *Colquhounia coccinea* bears soft, aromatic leaves and whorls of reddish-orange flowers on plants 2 m (7 ft) high in late summer and autumn. I have optimistically planted some *Echium fast-uosum,* but not with any great hope of them lasting through the winter. Raised from seed, they have made superb exotic-looking, 90 cm (3 ft) high, shrubby masses. The next plan is to try a spring planting of *Eucomis bicolor* (pineapple bulb), a good 15 cm (6 in) deep, and to try leaving this South African bulb out to fend for itself.

Where the border doubles back on itself to enclose a glade of grass, *Cea-nothus arboreus* 'Trewithen Blue' (capable of a height of 6 m (20 ft) and a spread of 8 m (26 ft), though frequently hit back by frost in colder areas), *Myrtus communis* 'Variegata', height and spread 3 m (10 ft), *Abies pinsapo* 'Glauca' (the Pinsapo fir), height 30 m (100 ft) and spread 3 m (10 ft), and *Cupressus sempervirens* 'Totem Pole', eventual height 15 m (50 ft) and spread 1.8 m (6 ft), a thin, columnar cypress, have been used to give structure. Between this lively assortment are various salvias, for some of which I have the insurance policy of overwintering cuttings in the greenhouse. Pink, ground-hugging diascia, *Osteospermum* 'Starlight' and *Helian-themum* 'Wisley Pink', with its superb mat of silvery leaves reaching a height of 20 cm (8 in) and spread 75 cm (2½ ft), have proved effective. Alpine plants like *Dryas octopetala,* height 6 cm (2.5 in) and spread indefinite, grown for its fluffy seed heads, and *Chaenorrhinum* 'Blue Dream' with its small, blue flowers, have made good carpets of growth. To fill gaps, annual *Ursinia anthemoides,* height 30 cm (1 ft) and spread 20 cm (8 in), has been valuable for its feathery leaves, shimmering, orange, daisy flowers and interesting seed heads.

The whole bed was mulched with an 8 cm (3 in) layer of shingle. As the pebbles are large, they have not become trodden all over the lawn and they boast another property. Even in drought, if you turn over a stone, there is usually moisture underneath. This layer of shingle seems to have trapped moisture in and kept competition from weeds down.

Directory of Drought Beaters

Dorycnium hirsutum

On a poor, dry soil, this attractive shrub is easy to grow. I took one cutting from a friend's plant, which rooted without trouble and now, four years later, is 60 cm (2 ft) in height and spread. The leaves are composed of three silvery-grey leaflets, which sets the whole bush shimmering, an effect augmented by small, white, pink-tinged pea-like flowers in summer. Small clusters of attractive, reddish, coloured fruits follow in autumn.

Eryngium bourgatii

This and other sea hollies are unusual, producing their silvery-blue, thistle-like flower heads in summer. These rise to 60 cm (2 ft) above a low rosette of handsome, deeply cut leaves which stay safely at ground level. The flower stems do have a tendency to sprawl about, but this is not unattractive in an informal setting.

Lavandula stoechas 'Marshwood'

This relatively new variety of French lavender was bred in New Zealand, along with 'Helmsdale'. French lavender is easily distinguished from other sorts by the bracts which stick up like rabbits' ears from the top of each flower head. In the case of 'Marshwood' these are an unusual brownish pink and in 'Helmsdale' are a strong, deep purple. They also have a rather astringent smell, which to me is far less pleasant than that of English lavender. There was a question mark over their hardiness, but they have survived hard winters in my dry soil without problem and have certainly not objected to summer drought. My plants have reached a height and spread of 75 cm (30 in). Treat as for normal lavender, allowing them to grow tall, or trimming them back in spring for more compact plants.

Nicotiana

There are few drought-tolerant bedding plants, but the doughty tobacco plants seem capable of tapping into moisture with their deep, thick roots. On my dry soil, they frequently act as perennials, bursting back into growth in spring. They all seem to share this advantage, as well as not appearing too regimented when added to informal plantings.

Pittosporum tenuifolium 'Irene Paterson'

This pretty evergreen will need a sheltered site but has proved itself worthy in my own garden by establishing well in a dry position and performing well during cold winters. Neat undulating leaves are mottled with sage green over a creamy background and contrast well with dark stems. New growth tends to be lighter, darkening with age. and older leaves can become tinged with pink in winter. A slow grower, it will eventually reach height 2.5 m (8 ft) and spread 1.5 m (5 ft).

Santolina chamaecyparissus

Cotton lavender bears dense shoots of close, silvery-grey leaves, joined in summer by small, round heads of yellow flowers on bushes up to a height and spread of 60 cm (2 ft). Cotton lavender is a valuable evergreen ideal for round, formal shapes as it can be clipped hard back in spring.

*Mixtures of colourful sedum, soft
grasses like* Stipa tenuissima *and silvery,
mat-forming plants such as helichrysum
and* Artemisia stelleriana *are set
off well by a shingle mulch. Add
an interesting bulb like tender*
Tulbaghia violacea
for the summer.

Tamarix tetrandra

For a plant of tree-like proportions, this shrub from Mediterranean areas is deep-rooted and tolerant of drought and saline soil. Green, needle-like foliage gives the shrub a very light appearance and the whole becomes a mass of pink in early summer when the flowers open. A height and spread of 3–4.5 m (10–15 ft) is normal, but pruning after flowering will keep growth in check.

Teucrium fruticans

The shrubby germander sprawls elegantly over the ground, its neat, aromatic, silvery leaves making a bright splash joined by lilac-blue flowers all summer. Expect a height of 90 cm (3 ft) and spread of some 1.2 m (4 ft).

Verbascum olympicum

This spectacular mullein is usually treated as a biennial, with seeds sown in spring making rosettes of large, felted, silvery leaves the first year. In their second summer, they rise up to produce branching spikes of furry buds opening to soft yellow flowers. Plants will seed themselves around and, reaching up to 1.8 m (6 ft), make imposing specimens.

Cottage-style Borders

~

Looking back in history, it is hard to see when the cottage style of gardening actually began. In the Middle Ages, anyone living in a hovel with a small piece of ground attached could have been described as a cottage gardener. Most peasants were so poor that it was in their own interests to grow vegetables and fruit,

This border really does illustrate the billowing which characterizes the cottage style. Shrubby hybrid rose 'Buff Beauty' sets the scene and plants have been allowed to mingle freely, but a controlling hand is needed to stop total anarchy.

~

plus, in some cases, herbs for use in medicine and hygiene. Cultivating flowers for pleasure in this context was mostly unheard of. Gradually, as time wore on, some folk became more prosperous, so that growing produce, flowers and herbs alongside foraging livestock was quite commonplace.

Gardening became more and more sophisticated as new plants entered the country from abroad and foreign gardening styles were copied in the gardens and estates of large houses. Some of these ideas filtered through to the gardens of poorer folk, who no doubt acquired some of the plants growing in their employers' gardens. There was also more movement of people between countries and foreigners brought their plants and ideas with them. While cottage gardeners copied the gentry, there was certainly an element of their being copied in return. Wealthy landowners enjoyed a romantic illusion of country life and built model villages to improve their outlook and cottages, complete with gardens, as retreats.

Cottage-style planting, though hard to define, is a mingling of semi-wild or wild-looking plants, sometimes growing with herbs and vegetables in a relaxed, flowing style perhaps punctuated by topiary and embraced by a perimeter of hedges or picket fencing. There has been recent criticism of the relentless copying of this style, instead of moving on to more modern gardening concepts. It would seem, however, that we cannot help ourselves. Our forbears were either forced, by necessity, to garden like this, or revelled in a more romantic and embellished copy of it. Either way, the cottage style seems to be a natural method of gardening with which we identify easily and feel at home.

Modern interpretations of the cottage gardening style vary considerably. Some gardeners are tidy-minded and create a pretty, cottage effect, using all the right plants, while retaining full control over them. To my mind, the most successful cottage gardens are where the owners have allowed the plants what appears to be full rein, only stepping in here and there to curb and restrain growth. To succeed with this, a full knowledge of the behaviour and habits of the plants is required.

I once looked after a cottage garden for three years while the owners were abroad. The design was typical, though not particularly clever and one felt that the garden had looked the same for at least a hundred years. A long, slender path flanked by narrow borders on both sides ran to the front door. On one side was a large lawn containing a rectangular rose bed, two large-clipped yew shapes and an old fish pond. The other side was a mixture of uneven crazy paving with small, irregular beds and the whole of the front garden was enclosed by hedges.

Apart from mowing the lawn, clipping the yews once a year in August and keeping the hedges under control, maintenance relied upon being able to tell weed seedlings from those of worthy plants. With cottage gardening, knowing when to step back and when to intervene is paramount. The rose bed needed pruning and weeding, but one of its glories was the perennial *Gypsophila paniculata,* height up to 75 cm (30 in) and spread 90 cm (3 ft), which grew beneath the roses. In summer it crept through their stems to open its froth of tiny, white flowers so that the blooms seemed wreathed in an everlasting bouquet. To complicate matters, the bottom tier of the bed was a carpet of violas. These had started as *V. tricolor,* the heartsease pansy, height and spread 5–15 cm (2–6 in), but had hybridized with other violas sending seedlings all over. These had to be retained to maintain the following year's display.

In the borders flanking the path, the first major display was from the huge clumps of catmint which reached up and then flopped all over the paths and lawn. If the old stems were cut away as soon as the flowers faded, these massive clumps would bloom again at the end of summer. They were backed by a superb display of hollyhocks which rose high, making a dramatic, tunnel-like effect leading to the front door. They were infested with rust, as many hollyhocks are, but as it happened only towards the end of their display, I ignored it. These, too, shed seed and because they are short-lived as perennials, new plants had to be left to take over from the old. The finale was the blooming of yellow *Achillea filipendulina* 'Gold Plate' with its aromatic, fern-like leaves and flat heads of yellow flowers rising to a height and spread of 1–1.2 m (3–4 ft). In all areas, weeding had to be undertaken carefully to maintain stocks of seedling *Myosotis* (forget-me-nots), *Aquilegia* (granny's bonnets), *Lychnis coronaria* (madam pinch-me-quick) and *Digitalis* (foxgloves)

growing under perennial favourites like delphiniums and phlox.

Cottage-style Border Plan

The front of the border pictured on page 114 will need full sun, but the back will tolerate and even enjoy some shade during the hottest parts of the day. A good medium loam will suit these plants which, apart from the lupins and ligularias, are quite drought-tolerant.

Pleasant shapes are shown off to perfection by the strong background formed here by a stone wall, the large leaves of ligularia and solid block of clipped hornbeam. Shapes that epitomize a cottage-style border are rounded or square blocks of clipped yew, box, hornbeam or other suitable plants, teamed with the spires of rising flower spikes. Here the rather formal standard rose is well complemented by blooms of salvia and lupins. Other key cottage-garden ingredients are present in the shape of silvery-leaved *Lychnis,* lavender and a mass of pretty sweet Williams. In order for the mositure-loving plants to surivive, I would make use of seep hoses laid on or just under the soil and attached to a tap. This way they can be easily watered during droughts.

Planning Cottage-garden Borders

There are some delightful and fragrant shrubs associated with the cottage style, which are indispensable in providing an outline for the border. The beauty of these informal shrubs is that they are

Planting Guide: page 115
Border Plan: page 113

While capturing the essence of typical herbaceous border style, this lively mixture of plants manages to be controlled as well as effective. It may not have the mad exuberance of some cottage borders, but it is a good example of this relaxed style.

among the easiest to grow. For spring flowers, the old-fashioned *Ribes sanguineum* (flowering currants) are hard to beat and will rise to a height of 1.8–2.75 m (6–9 ft). If the bright pinkish-red flowers are a little over-whelming, choose *R. s.* 'Tydeman's White', height and spread 2.5 m (8 ft), with clear white flowers. Some gardeners dislike the distinctive, rather pungent smell of flowering currants, but this should not disturb a sensitive nose if the shrubs are placed at the back of a border. *Syringa vulgaris* (common lilac) and its varieties are a more delicately perfumed choice and may reach up to 3.5 m (12 ft) on maturity. An unusual option guaranteed to provide a semi-wild appearance is *Rosa rubiginosa* (eglantine or sweetbriar). This rose will reach a height and spread of some 2.5 m (8 ft), bearing single, pink blooms in

Planting Guide (see page 114)

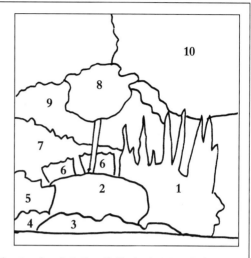

1. 3 x *Lupinus* (lupin), H: 1.2 m (4 ft), S: 60 cm (2 ft).

2. 3 x *Lavandula* 'Munstead', H and S: 60 cm (2 ft).

3. 5 x low-growing silver-leaved plant such as *Helichrysum italicum serotinum* (curry plant), H and S: 15 cm (6 in)

4. 3 x brightly coloured viola such as 'Jackanapes', H: 13 cm (5 in), S: 18 cm (7 in) or V. 'Johnny Jump Up'.

5. 9 x *Dianthus barbatus* (sweet William), H: 45 cm (18 in), S: 30 cm (1 ft).

6. 3 x *Lychnis coronaria* (madam pinch-me-quick), H: 45 cm (18 in), S: 30 cm (1 ft).

7. 3 x *Salvia nemorosa* 'May Night', H: 90 cm (3 ft), S: 45 cm (18 in).

8. *Rosa* 'Ballerina' as a standard, H: 1.5 m (5 ft), S: 75 cm (30 in).

Plot size: length 2.5 m (8 ft); depth 1.8 m (6 ft)

9. 3 x *Ligularia stenocephala*, H: 90 cm–1.8 m (3–6 ft) S: 75 cm (30 in).

10. *Carpinus betulus* (hornbeam), shape controlled by clipping.

early summer, followed by a good crop of red hips in autumn. Do not lose it right at the back of a border, as its chief delight is the sweetly aromatic foliage, which needs to be within reach.

For a small tree in a border, I would opt for *Amelanchier lamarckii* (snowy mespilus), height and spread 6 m (20 ft), for its white spring blossom and red autumn tints. Crab apples are attractive, too, with spring blossom followed by yellow, orange or red fruit which can be used for making jelly. Try *Malus* 'Dartmouth' with bright red fruit, or the popular *Malus* 'John Downie', both of which make small trees.

There are plenty of biennials and perennials for a spring show. *Doronicum* (leopard's bane) will bring a mass of yellow, daisy-like flowers to the middle of the border at 45 cm (18 in), with a liberal sprinkling of *Lunaria annua* (purple honesty), height 75 cm (30 in) and spread 30 cm (1 ft). *Pimpinella major* 'Rosea', the pink-flowered cow parsley is most attractive and reaches to 75 cm (30 in). *Anthriscus sylvestris* 'Ravenswing', height 75 cm (30 in) and spread 30 cm (1ft), is similar, with deep purple leaves and white flowers. For the front of a border, do not overlook yellow *Alyssum saxatile*, height 23 cm (9 in) and spread 30 cm (1 ft), white *Iberis sempervirens* and the various shades of aubrieta which have long been favourites. Clumps of daffodils, tulips and proud *Fritillaria imperialis* (crown imperial), height to 1.5 m (5 ft) and spread 23–30 cm (9–12 in), are important too. For dry soils, clumps of *Pulsatilla vulgaris* (pasque flower), height and spread 15–23 cm (6–9 in), will look superb and for slightly shady, moist positions, there are many primroses to try, from ordinary *Primula vulgaris,* height and spread 15–20 cm (6–8 in), to some of the beautiful double and gold-laced varieties.

For summer, aromatic, evergreen myrtle and rosemary can mingle with the perfumed flowers of *Philadelphus* (mock orange). These and roses will stage a setting for the performance of biennials and perennials massed in for a riot of colour. One rose variety repeated two or three times throughout the border will help tie in the rest of the plantings. I would opt for a soft peachy-pink colour like that of shrub rose 'Cornelia' or apricot-shaded 'Buff Beauty'. Tall *Campanula* (bellflowers) like *C. persicifolia,* which bears its blue or white flowers on stems reaching 1 m (3 ft), are ideal for furnishing the back of a border. Delphiniums, *Aruncus dioica* (goatsbeard), rising to 1.5 m (5 ft), *Leucanthemum* x *superbum* (syn. *Chrysanthemum maximum*) (dog daisy or shasta daisy), height 90 cm (3 ft) and spread 60 cm (2 ft), Hemerocallis (day lily) and tall *Kniphophia* (red hot poker) will make bold clumps too. For the front and middle of a border, *Polemonium caeruleum* (Jacob's ladder), height and spread 45–60 cm (18–24 in), *Papaver orientale* varieties (oriental poppies), *Geranium* 'Johnson's Blue' and *Centaurea cyanus* (cornflower), height 30–90 cm (1–3 ft) and spread 30 cm (1 ft), can hold sway. *Lysimachia punctata* is the familiar yellow-flowered plant, forming clumps some 60 cm (2 ft) round. By all means include it in a planting, but be aware that it spreads like wildfire if not kept in check. For spots of white and silver, choose *Achillea ptarmica* 'The Pearl', height 75 cm (30 in), or *Anaphalis triplinervis* (pearl everlasting) at 60 cm (2 ft).

To prevent borders from looking too orderly, with plantings graded neatly from tall at the back to short at the front, arrange a liberal sprinkling of plants throughout the depth of the border. Plant bulbs of *Allium sphaerocephalon* (a type of ornamental onion), height to 60 cm (2 ft) and spread 8–10 cm (3–4 in), *Lilium regale* (regal lily), height 50 cm–1.8 m (20 in–6 ft), to spring out as surprises. There can also be a wonderful mixture of self-seeded *Digitalis* (foxgloves), honesty, forget-me-nots and *Aquilegias* which appear throughout. Try unusual *Omphalodes linifolia,* height 15–30 cm (6–12 in) and spread 15 cm (6 in), which revels in the common name of Venus's navelwort.

Borders of Annuals and Tender Perennials

~

For many gardeners the time and expense of filling their borders with half-hardy annuals (those that cannot withstand frost) and tender perennials is justified by the colourful reward these plants bring. Most popular are summer bedding plants, bought during late spring by the trolley-load from garden centres, or grown from seed or small plants in the greenhouses of keen gardeners. Although economy is probably one of the main motives behind raising one's own plants, other advantages, apart from satisfaction, include having more control over choice of variety, particularly when it comes to selecting single colours to match and blend with each other.

Summer bedding is usually planted at the end of May (late spring) in most parts of the country. Frost would be unusual and there is a long growing season ahead, which allows the plants to reach maturity. To fill gaps left by summer bedding, there is a more restricted set of plants which can provide interest during autumn, winter or spring and sometimes all three. These plus spring bulbs are usually planted during autumn.

As well as filling whole borders with these seasonal plants, there is an increasing habit of using of them to plug holes in mixed borders, where they make more natural-looking drifts of colour. Alternatively, borders can be planted with tender plants, both annual and perennial, to create wonderfully sumptuous sub-tropical bedding which is great fun. By far the easiest and cheapest way to fill a border with quick colour is to direct sow seed of hardy annuals which requires only imagination and a few packets of seed.

Conventional Bedding for Borders

I know of several front gardens where the borders are a mass of bedding plants in summer and are left empty in winter. To me this a terrible shame, as my chief enjoyment of gardens is watching the change in plants from season to season. Most keen bedding plant growers choose feature or 'dot' plants to use as structure for their borders. They also select one or more types of plants to use as an edging. The rest of the space is filled in with colourful, middle-sized plants like *Petunia, Salvia, Geranium, Nicotiana* or marigolds graded by size and arranged at random, or made into circles or swirls of colours and types to form patterns. Suitable candidates for shady borders include *Fuchsia, Begonia, Mimulus* and *Impatiens*.

Tender perennials are often trained as standards to make effective, tall 'dot' plants whose stems can rise from a sea of smaller, colourful plants. Young, straight cuttings are grown tall and attached to a slender cane. Side shoots are removed until the desired height for a head of leaves and flowers is achieved. Side shoots are then encouraged to grow, with their tips pinched out to help more shoots develop, so making a rounded head of growth on top of a long stem. *Fuchsia* varieties are particularly good for this, especially those like 'Checkerboard', which naturally produce long, straight stems. Even some lax types like beautiful 'Jack Shahan' with its elegant, upturned pink sepals and darker pink skirt have strong stems which can be trained up to produce lovely, weeping standards. *Heliotrope,* too, makes a good standard with its head of hairy leaves and clusters of small, purple flowers with that individual fruity perfume, giving it the name cherry pie. Some varieties of *Argyranthemum* (marguerite), will produce heads of fern-like leaves and a profusion of daisy-like flowers.

Abutilon is often used as a dot plant, planted singly in small borders or in groups of three for large ones. Most popular has been *A. thompsonii,* height to 1.8 m (6 ft) and spread 90 cm (3 ft), with its virus-induced variegation of yellow on its maple-like leaves and a succession of bell-shaped, orange flowers. They are available with red, yellow or white flowers.

Seed-raised 'dot' plants can include sweetcorn, which fits in with the idea of using ornamental vegetables mixed with flowers. Another example is *Ricinus,* the true castor oil plant, which quickly grows into a tall specimen with large, exotic-looking, reddish-green leaves. Be careful how you handle the seeds, because they are highly poisonous. Also popular is the unusual *Kochia* or burning bush. Grown for its foliage this plant which resembles a small conifer turns a brilliant orange-red towards the end of summer and during autumn. Rising to 1–1.2 m (3–4 ft), *Cleome* or spider flower, makes an imposing sight with unusual pink flowers.

Edging plants, by their very nature, need to be compact and plant breeders have produced dwarf varieties of many different kinds of plants to try. *Lobelia* and *Alyssum* are traditional favourites, which now come in more colours than the original blue and white. There are lemon-coloured *Tagetes,* blue and white *Ageratum* with their fuzzy little flowers, *Begonia semperflorens* whose foliage is an attractive, shiny green or bronze contrasting with pink, red or white flowers and, for shady positions, *Impatiens.*

The Annual and Tender Perennials Border Plan

Bedding plants need good soil to grow well throughout the summer, so condition before planting in spring. Either add slow-release fertilizer just before planting, or plan to liquid feed regularly throughout the summer. A sunny aspect is needed for

Traditional tender perennials and half-hardy annuals have been used here to great and colourful effect against a backdrop of more mature planting.

~

Planting Guide: page 120
Border Plan: page 118

Planting Guide (see page 119)

1. 12 x *Ageratum,* H and S: 20 cm (8 in).
2. 9 x *Pelargonium,* H and S: 30 cm (1 ft).
3. 4 x Standard *fuchsia,* H: 1.2 m (4 ft), S: 75 cm (30 in).
4. 6 x *Pyrethrum* (now correctly *Tanacetum*) 'Silver Feather', H and S: 30 cm (1 ft).
5. 5 x *Begonia* 'Non-Stop', H and S: 25 cm (10 in).
6. *Hosta fortunei* 'Albopicta', H and S: 75 cm (30 in).
7. 5 x *Nicotiana* 'Lime Green', H: 75 cm (30 in), S: 45 cm (18 in).
8. *Prunus lusitanica,* trained as a standard.
9. *Photinia davidiana* 'Palette', H: 3 m (10 ft), S: 2.5 m (8 ft).
10. *Taxus baccata* 'Fastigiata Aurea', H: 1.8 m (6 ft), S: 30 cm (1 ft) in ten years, ultimately, H: 9 m (30 ft), S: 3.5 m (12 ft).

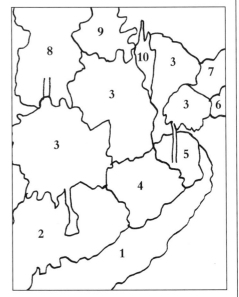

Plot size: length 5.5 m (18 ft); depth 1.8 m (6 ft)

the plants in the photograph on page 119 to do their best, though some, notably fuchsias and begonias, would tolerate shade.

Standard fuchsias have been used as the 'dot' plants in the border pictured on page 119. With care, they can be over-wintered in a frost-free environment and used year after year. They should be lifted in autumn and the roots tidied to fit them into large pots of loam-based pot-ting compost. At this stage the head can be trimmed back by half to two thirds. They must be given reasonably warm temperatures (minimum 4°C/40°F) or the stems of the head will die back. Some growers encase the long stems with pipe insulator. In early spring, as buds begin to show on the stems, trim the head back hard, but always leave short spurs of last year's stems behind. New growth will

burst forth, which can be shaped into a new head. When pinching back fuchsia shoots, remember they need about six weeks to grow and produce flower buds. On planting out, secure them to bamboo canes driven into the ground to hold the weight of leaves and flowers.

The edging is a ribbon of *Ageratum,* a reliable performer which should flower right through to the first frosts of autumn. It does better in dry weather, as constant rain tends to spoil the flowers. Within this, the fillers consist of solid groupings for impact. Seed-raised zonal *Pelargonium* (geranium), feathery silver *Pyrethrum* (now correctly *Tanacetum*) and double tuberous *Begonia* make effective blocks of colour. Notice how, further round the border where the bedding dis-play diffuses into shrub border, more gentle colours like *Nicotiana* 'Lime

Green' have been used. This tobacco plant has a more natural look and blends well with the foliage colours.

Filling gaps in mixed borders with annuals and tender perennials is how I prefer to use them. Blocks of *Petunia* against silver *Artemisia* 'Powis Castle', height 90 cm (3 ft) and spread 1.2 m (4 ft), or small groups of *Cosmos* 'Sonata', height 60 cm (24 in) and spread 45 cm (18 in), pushed in amongst herbaceous perennials here and there will augment the flowering display of a border throughout summer. If allowed to seed, they'll come up again by themselves the following year, bearing another crop of pink, red and white flowers above fern-like foliage.

Lavatera (mallows) are of a similar height and make a good display of glistening, saucer-shaped flowers. *Tithonia rotundifolia*, too, is a good plant for the back of a border, but allow plenty of room as just one specimen can reach 1.2 m (4 ft) high and some 90 cm (3 ft) wide. Again, the display of bright orange flowers on silky stems stretches into autumn. For a good gap filler with bright blue flowers, *Salvia farinacea* 'Victoria' is reliable, producing spikes of small, rich purple-blue flowers up to 45 cm (18 in) tall.

Subtropical Bedding

Subtropical bedding was a great hit in Victorian times, when head gardeners were able to overwinter all manner of exotic plants in their greenhouses and bed them out for the summer. Many of these were tender, shrubby perennials, which makes it hard for the average gardener, with limited greenhouse space, to copy. However, there are some imposing plants which can be raised annually from seed to create a similarly luxuriant effect.

Starting with tender perennials which can be kept going from year to year providing there is a heated greenhouse or conservatory to house them, there is the banana family. These really will transport you to the tropics and behave like giant tender herbaceous perennials. Unfortunately, they are unlikely to fruit when grown outside in the summer. The best type to choose is *Musa basjoo*, the Japanese banana, height 2 m (7 ft) and spread 1.5–1.8 m (5–6 ft), which is virtually hardy. In protected parts of the country it can be left outside in a sheltered position, thriving best against a wall or fence in well-drained soil. Close relative *Ensete ventricosum*, height 3 m (10 ft) and spread 1.8 m (6 m), produces lush foliage and is suitable to place outside for summer, but needs warm winter temperatures of 7°C (45°F) to do well.

Canna (Indian shot) is another good choice for conjuring up an illusion of the tropics. This can be raised from seed, but usually takes a few years to build up into an appreciable clump. The plants should be lifted from the ground at the end of each summer, potted up and left to die back in a greenhouse or shed. As long as they are frost-free and watered just occasionally so that the dormant rhizomes do not shrivel, they will start growing in spring. Then they need a light, well-ventilated frost-free place to grow on before planting out time in early summer. The

rewards are large leaves and tall spikes of exotic red, pink or yellow flowers.

Plants frequently grown as conservatory specimens, such as blue-flowered *Plumbago auriculata* (syn. *P. capensis*), with a height of up to 1.2 m(4 ft) and spread 60 cm (2 ft) with pruning and training, can have an alternative use as subjects for subtropical bedding. This also applies to the wonderful *Tibouchina urvilleana* (syn. *T. semidecandra*), height up to 1.8 m (6 ft) and spread 90 cm (3 ft) with pruning and training, known as Brazilian spider flower because the stamens in the centre of each huge, purple flower look like a spider lying on its back. Plants can easily be raised by seed or cuttings. *Abutilon* and orange-flowered *Streptosolen jamesonii*, height 1.8–3 m (6–10 ft), are also feasable stature plants. Most can be over-wintered just above freezing, or slightly warmer at 4°C (40°F).

Plants that can be raised from seed include *Ricinus* and *Eucalyptus*. The silvery juvenile foliage of young gum trees makes a lovely, foil to other colours. Keep them until they reach some 1.8–2 m (5–6 ft),

A mass of bloom can be created economically by sowing seeds of hardy annuals like Eschscholzia *(Californian poppy) and* Echium vulgare *(viper's bugloss) straight into the ground.*
~

Those who have greenhouse facilities to raise young plants from seed and overwinter tender perennials can create exotic-looking subtropical bedding. Here banana, Ricinus communis, Canna *'Striata',* Pelargonium *'Happy Thought',* Dahlia *'Bednall Beauty' and salvias have been used to great effect.*
~

then scrap and replace with a fresh batch. On a smaller scale, brightly coloured *Coleus* and dark-leaved *Perilla* make bold additions. Some of the newer *Salvia* varieties like *S.* 'Lady in Red' have exotic appeal. Add to them some hardy herbaceous perennials like *Lobelia cardinalis* (cardinal flower) with its bronze-purple foliage and spikes of bright red flowers for extra impact. This *Lobelia*, which can rise to 90 cm (3 ft), likes plenty of moisture, so be ready to water during droughts. *Verbena bonariensis* is easy to raise from seed and in most soils and locations will return again year after year. The tall stems of rosy lavender flowers are lovely, rising to 1.2-1.5 m (4–5 ft).

OXFORD
UNIVERSITY PRESS

Great Clarendon Street, Oxford, OX2 6DP, United Kingdom

Oxford University Press is a department of the University of Oxford.
It furthers the University's objective of excellence in research, scholarship,
and education by publishing worldwide. Oxford is a registered trade mark
of Oxford University Press in the UK and in certain other countries

British Library Cataloguing in Publication Data
Data available

ISBN: 978-0-19-835651-6

10 9 8 7 6 5

Paper used in the production of this book is a natural, recyclable product
made from wood grown in sustainable forests. The manufacturing process
conforms to the environmental regulations of the country of origin.

Printed in China by Golden Cup

Acknowledgements

Series Advisor: Nikki Gamble

Chapter 1

The train stopped.

Eva sighed. It was a long journey and they were nearly there. She was really looking forward to seeing her grandad. "The train can't stop now!" she said. "What's happened?"

"I don't know," her mum replied. "We'll probably start moving again soon. Why don't you do something like … write a story?"

Eva looked at the blank page in front of her. She could hear the rain tapping at the train window.

"I don't know what to write," Eva said.
"I can't think of anything."

Suddenly, the driver's voice came over a loudspeaker. "I'm very sorry," he said. "The railway line is broken. We have to stay here until it's fixed. It's going to take quite a while."

Oh no …

What about Grandad?

"Wh–what's going on?"

"I can't believe it!"

"I'll be late!"

"That's a shame!" sighed Mum. "Why don't you start your story while we're waiting, Eva? I'll phone Grandad."

Eva looked again at her blank page.

"Just start writing," said Mum gently. "See what happens."

So Eva started writing. She read aloud as she wrote.

Once there was a boy called Luca.
He wanted to go on an adventure.

Luca had a little dog
called Ticket!

"Right. Where might Luca and Ticket be going?"
Eva asked herself out loud.

TREASURE FOUND!

"Maybe they're going to find some …
treasure," said the man in the next seat.
"Treasure!" said Eva. "That's a good idea!"

Luca and Ticket were going to find some treasure.

They lived in a village where it rained all the time.
It had rained every single day for years and years.
This made everyone in the village very sad.

One day, Luca and Ticket were walking in the rain when they saw Luca's favourite bookshop.

It was the perfect place to shelter from the storm.

The shop was full of old books and maps.

"Come in out of the rain, Luca," said the shopkeeper. "Isn't this weather horrible?"

"Maybe one day someone will find the missing **treasure** and cheer us all up!" the shopkeeper continued.

"Treasure?" asked Luca excitedly.

Ticket was excited, too.

"Yes. People say there's a **huge** chest of gold hidden somewhere!" explained the shopkeeper.

She told them the treasure had been buried by a giant!

"A giant?" said Luca.

"Yes," replied the shopkeeper. "If only someone would find the gold — that would cheer everyone up in this rainy village!"

"We'll find it, won't we?" Luca said to Ticket. "Let's go!"

"Be careful," said the shopkeeper. "When you
find the treasure, you might find the giant, too!"
"We aren't scared, are we, Ticket?" said Luca.

16

The shopkeeper rushed after them and gave Luca a map.

"Good luck!" she said.

Luca looked at the map.

"First, we have to go through this forest," he said.

It was dark and creepy in the forest and Luca suddenly felt a bit scared. Ticket led the way, wagging her tail.

Chapter 3

At the end of the forest, Luca and Ticket came to a mountain!

They climbed right to the top of the mountain.

They rested there, in the pouring rain.

Luca wiped the rain from his eyes and looked at the map.

They had to cross the sea,
so they needed to find a boat!

"Where will we find a boat,
up here?" thought Luca.
Suddenly, Ticket spotted a boat
down the other side of the mountain.

Luca and Ticket rushed down the mountain and climbed into the boat. They rowed off into the waves.

At last, they landed on a sandy beach. "Look, over there!" Luca cried, pointing to an **enormous 'X'** marked in the sand.

"But what about the treasure?" said Luca. "This is just an old key!" He looked up and saw a lighthouse!

"The key must fit the lighthouse door!" yelled Luca, and they ran to see.

Luca unlocked the door and it creaked open.
"Is anyone there?" he whispered.
All he could see was a long trail of wool!

Chapter 4

Luca picked up the end of the wool.
His heart was beating very fast.
He felt scared but excited.

"Come on, Ticket," he said.
"Let's see where this wool
leads."

They followed the wool all over the lighthouse.
They went up the stairs,
and in and out of enormous rooms.

In the end it led them to ...

The giant was sitting on the floor. He looked worried. He was wearing a **big** jumper that was coming undone. Luca took a deep breath.

"Please," he said to the giant. "Can you show me where the treasure is?"

"I'm sorry," said the giant. "There is no treasure!
Please don't be cross. I told people I had hidden
the treasure so someone would come here. I was
lonely and I just wanted someone to talk to."

Luca, Ticket and the giant came out
of the lighthouse into the rain.
    "Can't you stay?" asked the giant.
"Just for a cup of tea?"
    "Sorry," said Luca.
"I'm wet and tired.
I just want to
go home."

"Wait! I've got an idea that will help you," said the
giant. He took a deep breath and ... blew the clouds away!

The sun came out. It dried Luca's clothes and fluffed up Ticket's fur.

Luca smiled at the giant. "You've done it! You've brought back the sunshine!" he cried. "Come back to the village with me! Everyone will want to thank you!"

So they raced all the way back to the village.

When they got back, the village was shining
in the bright sun.

"This giant blew away the rain!" Luca said
to the villagers.

"Hooray!" everyone shouted.

They all had a picnic in the sunshine to celebrate. "This is better than treasure!" said Luca, smiling.

Finally, the train stopped at the station.

"Goodbye!" Eva called to all the other passengers. "Thanks for all your ideas!"

She jumped off the train and ran over to where her grandad was waiting.

"Grandad," she said, hugging him tightly, "do you want to hear a story?"